Copyright

A catalogue record for this book is available at the South African National Library.

ISBN 0-620-24356-2

Designed by
The Design Council
Attic Rush

Printed and bound in South Africa.
Reproduction by Hirt and Carter, Durban.

Contents

Foreword

By Ian McIntosh

As many of you will know this has been my last season as coach of the Natal Sharks. For both myself and the team, despite many upheavals, it turned out to be a most enjoyable year, culminating in a Currie Cup final.

It was an unusual request when Paul and Sean came to us and asked for permission to follow us around, but after setting some ground rules, we agreed.

It was a pleasure to have them along with us, and even though we thought we had lost them in Australia they stuck doggedly to the task. It says something for their commitment to the project that they were with us at all the large venues, but also turned up at the smaller venues such as Welkom, Wellington and George.

Unobtrusive and always polite they gained the trust and confidence of the team as the photographs will show. It's policy not to allow people into the change room yet Sean in particular almost became part of the furniture, never getting in the way and always remaining discreet.

I hope you enjoy Black & White — A Season With The Sharks as much as we enjoyed having the guys with us.

Introduction

It seemed like a good idea, though my wife would disagree. Follow the Natal Sharks around for an entire season. Not just any old season, but 1999. The end of a decade, the threshold of a millennium, and for Natal Sharks fans the end of an era.

In a decade Natal have gone from being the fun-loving, perennially under-achieving Banana Boys to the ruthlessly successful Sharks. As a team they have dominated South African rugby during the 90's to record four Currie Cup victories.

The man responsible for this turnaround in fortune has been Ian McIntosh. His force of personality and absolute passion for rugby has translated itself not only to the players who work under him, but the entire province. People love the Sharks, they love going to the game, they have loved being part of the success.

But the real reason was a chance to document the close of a triumphant chapter in Natal rugby history, and from a purely personal point of view, get to spend nine months watching rugby.

From a historical point of view 1999 had a lot going for it. It was commonly thought that it would be Mac's (we called him Mr McIntosh the first time we met him but he insists on Mac) last season, as well as a swansong for heroes such as Gary Teichmann, Henry Honiball and André Joubert.

Sean and I, please note they spelt his name wrong on his accreditation, are first and foremost Sharks fans. *Black & White — A Season With The Sharks* is simply about them and I apologise for any naked, unreasoning bias that comes through in both the pictures and the narrative.

Throughout the year we have had our credentials questioned, been refused entry, been ushered to the front of the queue, seen the team in triumph and defeat, wanted to shout but held back as we maintained journalistic integrity, travelled thousands of miles to follow the team, drunk many beers in celebration and a few in defeat, been introduced to Red Bull and vodka, spent time with men considered heroes by many, and more importantly witnessed at first hand every moment of this epic season.

While we both have sporting backgrounds this book hasn't been put together from a traditional sports-journalism perspective. We looked at things as die-hard fans, with the skewed perspective this brings.

As far as South African rugby is concerned nobody has been behind the scenes with both camera and pen and we are grateful to the Natal Rugby Union for giving us the chance to do this.

We have attempted to show things a little differently, to show what goes on behind the scenes without infringing on the players privacy. We have tried to provide a fresh insight into the workings of a professional rugby team. We hope you enjoy it as much as we did.

Paul Mitchell

5
vodacom
1999
5

Pre-season

January 1999 is the hottest in 30 years and at 7am the temperature is already in the mid 20's. Early season training is not pleasant, it's not meant to be. The squad train six days a week under the direction of fitness adviser Kevin Stevenson who fulfils the same role for the Springboks.

The routines and drills are aimed at building endurance and conditioning as a secure and solid fitness base. Routines range from a punishing early morning swim around the piers at North Beach to specialised gym routines at the La Lucia and Kings Park Health & Racquet Clubs. Power circuits underneath the main stand in the morning are followed in the afternoon by skills and fitness training.

Twice a week the squad pound up-and-down North Beach between the piers doing punishing running and swimming circuits. Up the beach, along the pier, a jump into the sea, swim to shore, back along the beach and then wade out into the waves before swimming back.

Kevin calls it a natural work-out: "The sea is right on our doorstep, so we might as well make use of it."

Kevin leads from the front closely followed by Mark Andrews and assistant coach Hugh Reece-Edwards.

This season the "loaners", players from other unions, manage to stay out of trouble and there are no repeats of last year's near drowning incidents. It is unlike anything they have experienced before though and they struggle. The big props Brent Moyle, Baksteen Nel and Morné van der Merwe are a lumbering presence at the back.

There is a determination and intensity about training that is fuelled by the disappointment of last season's glorious, yet futile, semi-final failures as well as professional pride.

The Super 12 is the premier southern hemisphere provincial competition and one in which the players would like some success. The Sharks have so far been the only South African side to have performed

Above: *Running south towards Addington and South Beach*
Opposite: *Warren Brosnihan*
Previous page: *Leap of faith. The jump off the pier with the hotels of North Beach in the background.*

with any credibility in the Super 12 and after last season's narrow loss to the Crusaders in the semi, 36-34, they probably feel that some reward is due them.

By late-January the intensity begins to build and this is reflected in the way the squad go about their work. Coach Ian McIntosh constantly expresses the need for explosiveness in everything they do. In the modern game it is punishing pace over the first five yards, that will send you through a gap or send an attacker backwards as he is tackled.

The intensity is obvious in what seem the more mundane fitness exercises. There is intense competition between team-mates with the more noticeable and serious attempts at one-upmanship among the forwards.

From a simple step exercise to a game of touch rugby there is a passionate competitive under-current. Each player, like all professional sportsmen, has a sense of self-belief that translates naturally into on-field arrogance; an absolute necessity for success no matter what sport you play.

As Ollie Le Roux says when talking about the

Above: *Stefan Terblanche, after an impressive Super 12 season for the Sharks in 1998 is back in Durban for good.*
Far right: *Soon to be one of the finds of the season, South African Under 21 captain John Smit*
Right: *Hooker Mornay Visser practices his throwing in.*

up-coming Super 12, "It's a great competition. You play against the best and some guys even think they are better than you."

Conspicuous by their absence are the Springboks, Gary Teichmann, Pieter Muller, Henry Honiball and Adrian Garvey. The extended 1998 season has taken its toll on them and they are all given a little extra time to recover. In the case of Pieter and Adrian both have had surgery, on shoulder and achilles respectively.

The coaching staff are always there cajoling, admonishing and encouraging — equally fit and equally committed. While the back-up staff is not as vast as other Super 12 teams, our cousins down south spring to mind, it has been carefully picked.

Team manager Allister "Webster" Coetzee is from Eastern Province and works closely with team director/jack-of-all-trades Mike Kelroe-Cooke. They manage all the logistics with the assistance of Mac's secretary Meryl Cleal and team travel organiser Terri Curtis.

The doctor, Glen Hagemann and physiotherapists Dave Becker and Steve Felsher are close in age to the players so there is a relaxed informal attitude throughout the squad.

Subtle changes to the legendary McIntosh/Sharks direct style are discussed.

The squad is blessed with a lot more speed out wide this season and Mac is determined to utilise that. On top of that the wings have been complaining that they don't get enough ball, a constant and familiar complaint to anyone that has played rugby.

Duncan Robertson, formally a coach at Otago and an ex-All Black has also been flown over from New Zealand at Mac's request to provide a fresh perspective with particular emphasis on the back-line. He has been closely involved with Otago, 1998 New Zealand National Provincial Champions, and toured South Africa in 1976 with the All Blacks

In addition to all the physical work there are two sets of lectures a week over breakfast. Referee Jonathan Kaplan helps the players as they try to get to grips with yet more law changes and the myriad interpretations while there is naturally plenty of emphasis on tactics and game plans.

The players are quite vocal at these sessions as they seek ways to cut down on their error base. The sessions are not all criticism and plenty of video footage is shown of positive, successful rugby. It is noticeable that attention is paid to any weaknesses of the Sharks, not on the strength of their opponents.

While Mac, naturally, has the final say everyone, especially the players, has vital and valid input. The sense of trust, a hallmark of Mac's management style, that this encourages, is tangible.

The team skills and practice sessions are held in the afternoon and usually last no longer than an hour-and-a-half. Intensity and concentration are drummed into the players. Train as you want to play.

Mistakes are invariably highlighted in acerbic and precise fashion by Mac: "Unlucky Deon unlucky, do it again and you can piss off home."]

Left: *Mac and Duncan Robertson plot the downfall of their opponents or discuss where their next round of golf is going to be.*

Right: *There are tyres on the end of the ropes. To end a training session the players get to do a couple of lengths of the field.*

Reebok
SHARKS
Reebok

Reebok
Reebok
Reebok
Strapping

Eastern Cape

The team fly into Port Elizabeth on February 11 and travel by coach to Cape St Francis. They split up into chalets and have to fend for themselves. It's enlightening but don't expect a celebrity Shark cookbook any time soon.

The week away includes two warm-up games against Eastern Province and Border Invitational XV's but is more important as an exercise in team building and bonding. As well as finalising tactics and working on match skills there are talks from motivational speaker Anton van der Post, and intense tactical talks from Mac which he illustrates with complex post-impressionist drawings.

But there is also a lot of free time — and rugby players get bored very easily. Like many top sportsmen they are more than competent at most sports and like a wager or a forfeit if no money is to hand. Volleyball, tennis, golf, one-bounce you name it. There is also jet-skiing and quad bikes and blowing the traditional image of rugby players right out of the water — chess.

At the Fish River Sun there is a volleyball tournament with the enticing incentive of hotel T-shirts for the winners. The competition is intense with Mark Andrew's team making full use of his height to claim the prestigious trophy.

There is also a thriving card school which operates an interesting forfeit system and in keeping with tradition the odd beer in the evening to soothe the soul and keep the muscles well-oiled.]

From top:

A Rolls Royce, a man and his dog - André Joubert takes a breather during training in Port Alfred;

The Grandmasters - John Smit and Nico Wegner intent on their chess match;

Half-back surprise - Chad Alcock prepares supper for his flatmates;

John Slade forfeits in his usual exuberant fashion after losing at cards.

***Right:** The Sharks draw crowds wherever they go. This family spent the afternoon watching them train at Cape St. Francis.*

FLOWERS
FLOWERS

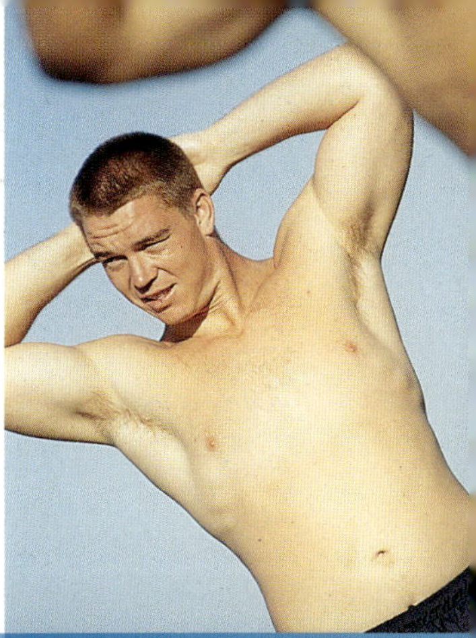

Opposite: *Mark Andrews climbs above Wayne Fyvie.*
Above: *Stephen Brink goes for a spin on a quad bike.*
From top right:
John Smit has a bit of a flex in a desperate attempt to get a tan;
Hugh Reece-Edwards celebrates a vital point;
Heated action in the preliminary matches.
Below: *Morné van der Merwe (left) and Jacques Greef exhibit previously unimagined tennis skills.*
Next page: *The squad pose after training.*

ored By
ADIO & TV
Reebok

PLASCON
We Surface
Everywhere
NATAL
Reebok

Super 12

In the second week of February the 'official' Super 12 squad is announced on Boots And All and manages to differ significantly from the "real official" squad announced at a sponsored breakfast the next day.

The Super 12 is the premier provincial competition in world rugby and is played at the beginning of the season between four South African, three Australian and four New Zealand sides. Each side plays the others once with the top four going through to the semi-finals. Four points are awarded for a win with a bonus point for scoring four or more tries, and one for a losing side finishing within seven points of the opposition. In three years of competition the Sharks have appeared in two semi-finals and one final.

In televised interviews Mac looks and sounds the most relaxed of all the South African coaches. The immensely likable Eugene Van Wyk of the Bulls, under intense pressure with a long injury list and inadequate replacements, seems close to developing a nervous tic. The Stormers Alan Solomons looks more shifty and evasive than usual and André Markgraaf of the Cats is his usual affable, lovable self.

For the Sharks the anticipation and accompanying nervousness of the up-coming first game of the season is exacerbated by a long injury list and the feeling that it is much too early for the season to start, a feeling compounded by the intense heat and lack of rain. On top of the missing Teichmann, Honiball, Garvey and Muller, there is a major scare on Wednesday before the game when full-back André Joubert is stung by a bee and suffers a bad allergic reaction. Thankfully he is treated quickly and is fit for the game.

The over-riding feeling is that for a change the Sharks are going into a home game as the underdogs. The Waratahs are expected to do well after three disappointing seasons and are considered the best of the Australian sides. They have no injury worries and, unlike the Sharks, have already played a couple of tough warm-up games.

SHARKS
Reebok

vs Waratahs

***The Sharks 13 NSW Waratahs 13**, The Stadium Kings Park, Durban. 27 February 1999*

***Sharks:** Joubert, Terblanche, Gillingham, Payne, Swart, Benadé, Alcock, McLeod-Henderson, Fyvie, Andrews, Atherton, van Rensburg, Le Roux, Rossouw, Smit*

***Waratahs:** McCrae, Jones-Hughes, Little, Grey, Staniforth, Warner, Whitaker, Strauss, Pinkerton, Welborn, Bowman, Brial, Blades, Kearns, Harry*

The Sharks team contains some surprises; at scrum-half Alcock gets the nod ahead of Martens and John Smit is preferred to Brent Moyle. Brad McLeod Henderson, somewhat surprisingly, is preferred at No 8 to Warren Brosnihan while Wayne Fyvie takes over the captaincy.

The temperature is in the high 20's and humidity is dense. The Sharks start well and the noise, as Joubert sends a kick pirouetting into touch, is raucous and encouraging. Benadé puts over a penalty while Warner and Edmonds miss relatively simple kicks. The Waratahs lose a lineout outside their 22, Andrews picks up the loose ball and bursts through. He pops up a pass inside and Fyvie is there to score.

Crucially the Sharks lose concentration before half-time. Fly-half Christian Warner runs blind and beats the desperate tackles of Alcock and Joubert to go over in the corner. The Sharks seem to be battling with the heat. Andrews is replaced by Brosnihan after 60 minutes which takes away the last bit of fire from the pack.

Fyvie leads from the front but the tight five keep coming in last at the breakdown. At a maul the Sharks wait for the whistle as Whitaker breaks and puts Jones-Hughes away. He falls short of the line but the Waratahs win the ball back and Whitaker goes over with the defence in tatters.

The Waratahs miss the conversion so the scores remain level. To their credit the Sharks spend the last five minutes in the opposition 22. They come close to pinching it when Joubert floats a kick into the corner, but Terblanche knocks-on in the air.

A draw is probably a fair result and Mac seems relieved, though not particularly full of smiles. The Sharks performed well below par yet still managed to contain the highly rated Aussies.]

Above: *Waratah centre Nathan Grey passes to lock John Welborn as he is tackled by Sharks captain Wayne Fyvie.*

10

vs Brumbies

***The Sharks 21 ACT Brumbies 15**, Telkom Park, Port Elizabeth, 5 March*
***Sharks**: Joubert, Pedro, Gillingham, Kayser, Terblanche, Honiball, Alcock, Teichmann, van Rensburg, Fyvie, Andrews, Atherton, Smit, Rossouw, Le Roux*
***Brumbies**: Kafer, Hardy, Magro, Holbeck, Mortlock, Larkham, Gregan, Falcon, Robinson, Giffen, Harrison, Williams, Noriega, Paul, Young*

The constant wind of Port Elizabeth provides a pleasant change from the heat of Durban. A nice man stands outside the main entrance to Telkom Park and hands out envelopes containing tickets — welcome to rugby the way it used to be.

The field is set in a bowl and has the potential to be an intimidating arena. Sadly the stadium itself looks as if the omnipresent wind may bring it crashing down onto the pitch at any moment. There is a ten minute queue to get into the main stand as there is only one lift and no other way of getting up three storey's. Despite these minor inconveniences there is no doubt that the 20 000 strong crowd are firmly behind the Sharks.

The Sharks have made four changes to their side. Gary Teichmann returns in place of Brad McLeod-Henderson, Henry Honiball for Benadé and local hero Henry Pedro for the injured Justin Swart. Deon Kayser starts in the centre in place of Shaun Payne. ACT are tough competitors but their discipline was poor against the Cats the week before. They have one of the most exciting backlines in the competition and always pose a threat, particularly with the ball in hand. The Sharks again start well but go 6-0 behind to two Stirling Mortlock penalties. After 15 minutes a simple backline move makes space for Joubert who takes the gap and hands off to Terblanche who goes over in the corner.

Despite this lead Joubert is missing his kicks which

***From left:** Chad Alcock, Charl van Rensburg and Gary Teichmann close down Stephen Larkham.*

means that constant Sharks pressure goes unrewarded. They then run a free kick close to the Brumbies line and send Le Roux into space but he knocks-on as he goes over the line. The Brumbies move down the field and are awarded a series of scrums five metres out. A problem on the tight head eventually sees the referee award a penalty try against the Sharks for continual infringement. The score is now 5-13.

Pedro goes off with a recurrence of ligament strain, which will end his season, while Wayne Fyvie follows shortly with an elbow injury. Payne and Brosnihan come on to replace them.

The performance is a mixed bag. The Sharks are playing with confidence but keep losing the ball in contact. They make decisive bursts but then fail to make the advantage pay.

Honiball takes over the kicking and gets the score back to 8-15. Early in the second-half Gillingham breaks down the blind side and throws a big dummy before going over under the posts. Another penalty gives them the lead but ACT still threaten.

Despite dominating, the continuing catalogue of small errors of judgement mean that it remains a tight game and the Sharks once again miss out on a vital bonus point. The Sharks defence is impressive and things can't be too bad if they can win while playing at about 70%.]

Right: *Local support.*

Far right: *An exuberant performance from local Xhosa dancers made for slightly different and more energetic than usual pre-match entertainment.*

Below: *André Joubert, John Smit and Gary Teichmann warm up before the game.*

Below left: *Chris Rossouw quenches his thirst during a break in the game.*

Reebok
Reebok
Canon
Canon

vs Cats

***The Sharks 36 The Cats 20**, Ellis Park Stadium, Johannesburg, 13 March*

***Sharks:** Joubert, Terblanche, Gillingham, Payne, Brink, Honiball, Martens, Teichmann, Fyvie, Andrews, Atherton, Van Rensburg, Moyle, Visser, Le Roux*

***Cats:** Kruger, vd Walt, Van Jaarsveld, Mulder, Venter, O'Neill, Swanepoel, Venter AJ, Venter, Matfield, Smit, Erasmus, Heymans, Drotske, Groenewald*

The Cats are the errant sons of South African rugby - the quintessential black sheep of the family. Gifted but endlessly disappointing, talented yet undermined by petulance and indiscipline. This season they have been given every chance to do well but have been unable to rid themselves of fundamental flaws.

Coach André Markgraaf epitomises their problems as he attracts controversy wherever he goes. In the run up to this game it is the refusal of Hennie Le Roux to play for the Cats after he was dropped following a minor injury earlier in the season.

They line up against the Sharks hobbled by injuries, indifference and petty squabbles. Feeling even more confident after the splendid treatment from the Cats/Lions media liaison people it is something of a surprise to see the Sharks 13-0 down after 15 minutes. They look slightly bemused and not even warmed up. The huge downpour which arrives just as the teams take the field enhances the bedraggled look.

But then it starts to work, as Gary Teichmann says later, "I didn't have to tell the guys what to do. They all knew what their jobs were. They didn't panic and just stuck to the plan we talked about beforehand."

Henry Honiball puts over three penalties and the Cats are unable to get out of their own half. In the 34th minute there is a moment of vintage Sharks, a move last seen in the Currie Cup-winning 1996 season. A scrum in the Cats 22, a quick heel and as Martens peels out to the open side, Teichmann passes to Joubert on the blind side who grubbers through for Stephen Brink to pick up and score in the corner. Honiball converts from close to the touch line and the Sharks take a 16-13 lead into the break.

Immediately after the re-start Honiball makes a break after a line out and feeds Joe Gillingham. The ball is recycled twice and moves right where Steve Atherton, lurking in the tramlines, goes over for his first Super 12 try. To balance this personal triumph he is later sent to the sin-bin for punching, in retaliation let it be said.

With the Sharks on the attack Lourens Venter intercepts and races 60 metres to score under the posts. Stepping up a gear the Sharks defend well, although a man short, and once more push the Cats back upfield. Honiball kicks two more penalties to put the game out of the Cats reach.

With minutes remaining Ollie Le Roux peels off from a lineout, pops the ball up to John Slade, who adds to his cult hero status by scoring. Mac is grinning afterwards and must shake every journalist by the hand. After all, it's not often you get two tries from your locks.]

***Right:** Mark Andrews goes high into the rain to contest possession.*

Below:

Ollie le Roux leads the charge;

It was a wet and stormy night.

SHARKS
Reebok
Canon

Reebok

NATAL
Reebok
Reebok

Canon

vs Highlanders

***The Sharks 32 vs Otago Highlanders 8**, The Stadium Kings Park, Durban, 26 March*
***Sharks:** Joubert, Terblanche, Payne, Gillingham, Brink, Honiball, Martens, Teichmann, Fyvie, Andrews, Atherton, van Rensburg, Moyle, Visser, Le Roux*
***Highlanders:** Wilson, Laney, Stanley, Alatini, Lima, Culhane, Kelleher, Maka, Kronfeld, Blaikie, Timmins, Randell, Meeuws, Oliver, Hoeft*

The Sharks have a two week break giving sore bodies the chance to recover properly but there is the worry that any momentum built by the Cats victory may be dissipated by the pause.
"It's all I've been able to think about for the past week " says Joe Gillingham, "I just want to play, it's on my mind as I fall asleep and as soon as I wake up in the morning."
Otago scraped a victory against the Cats the week before but are still widely tipped to win the tournament. The Sharks and Highlanders seem to bring out the best in each other as previous encounters have seen some of the highest scoring games in the tournament.
Both teams are at full-strength but they start cautiously. An early Honiball penalty is matched by Culhane. Both sides are kicking away a lot of ball and seem to be weighing each other up. The Sharks have the territorial edge and look to be the more fluent side.
Otago scrum-half Byron Kelleher is making a lot of ground around the fringes but doesn't always have the support as Wayne Fyvie manages to keep Kronfeld quiet.
John Smit comes on to replace Brent Moyle mid-way through the first half and immediately makes his presence felt in the loose.
With five minutes remaining in the first half a big drive from the forwards sees Mark Andrews go over with Honiball converting. Crucially, just before the break, the Sharks score again. Otago have just had inside-centre Pita Alatini sent to the sin-bin for an off-the-ball tackle although replays show that it was Joe Stanley who committed the foul.
Quick ball off-the-top of a lineout gives Honiball the time to make a break outside his opposite number and exploit Alatini's absence. He slips a pass to Gillingham who is inside on his shoulder. Joe has a clear run to the line and goes over under the posts. The try is converted and the Sharks go in at the break 17-3 up.
The Sharks come out firing after the break and quickly add another penalty. They start to apply a lot of pressure with scrum-half Hentie Martens lifting his game to match the excellent Kelleher
The Sharks start to throw the ball around and are soon rewarded with another try. John Smit makes a superb pick-up off his toes and sets up a ruck on the Otago line. Ollie Le Roux gets his hands on the ball and forces himself over. Honiball converts and Otago are now out of the game.

"We got a hiding, we didn't fire a shot."
Otago coach Tony Gilbert

The Otago pack is still impressive in set play but they are taking a beating in the loose. Young John Smit is incredibly mobile and constantly makes himself available to carry the ball up. He also throws in a dummy and a couple of one-handed passes to let Jeff Wilson know he isn't the only showman on the field.
Deon Kayser comes on for Stephen Brink and immediately makes an impression with a couple of big cover tackles. The Sharks are beginning to throw the ball around recklessly as they look for the elusive first bonus point

of the season.

Towards the end both teams are looking exhausted but the intensity doesn't drop. Finally in the last minute the ball is moved along the backline one last time. André Joubert makes room and Stefan Terblanche goes over in the corner. The bonus point is secured to send 35 000 people home smug and happy.

Afterwards Otago coach Tony Gilbert is frank and open in his appraisal of his team's performance : "We got a hiding, we didn't fire a shot. The try before half-time killed us off."

When asked who impressed him most in the Sharks line-up he was equally direct, "They were moving so fast I couldn't tell you." Mac is a little more circumspect : "I'm very happy to have beaten such a good side but I was disappointed that we didn't capitalise on our good start. We also kicked too much and gave away too much ball which wasn't part of our plan."

But as Mac is so fond of saying, you can't plan the Super 12.]

Above far right: *Joe Gillingham celebrates his crucial score just on half-time.*

Above centre: *Mac and Hugh Reece-Edwards watch nervously.*

Right: *Australian referee Wayne Erickson had his hands full keeping the two front-rows honest. Mornay Visser and Ollie le Roux get ready to meet the All Black trio Meeuws, Oliver and Hoeft head on.*

Below: *Henry Honiball gets to grips with his opposite number, Simon Culhane.*

Winfield

Canon
GILLINGHAM
12

adidas

Reebok
Canon

vs Hurricanes

***The Sharks 18 vs Wellington Hurricanes 34**, Basil Kenyon Stadium, East London, 3 April*
***Sharks:** Joubert, Terblanche, Payne, Gillingham, Brink, Honiball, Martens, Teichmann, Fyvie, Andrews, Atherton, Van Rensburg, Smit, Visser, Le Roux*
***Hurricanes:** Cullen, Umaga, Ieremia, O'Halloran, Telea, Holwell, Spice, Fale, Vanisi, Falaniko, Afeaki, Blowers, Slater, Hewitt, Tuirangi*

A friend at university once described East London as the ghost by the coast, an apt description for this forlorn would-be city. And I should point out that he came from Bulawayo, hardly the cradle of Southern African civilisation. This is meant to be a home game but on arrival the night before André Joubert remarks that it's even worse than being in Palmerston North, condemnation indeed.

In their wisdom the fixture committee has moved the game away from a full-to-the-brim Durban on Easter weekend and put it in East London. The chartered plane lands in freezing mist on Good Friday evening. Team manager Allister is roundly abused for insisting on shorts as that day's uniform.

Saturday is cloudy, then rainy, then boiling hot. We take a walk around town and find ourselves at 'ye olde town gaol' which has been delightfully re-invented as a poky shopping centre. I think it was more cheery when it was still a gaol. A couple sitting outside this 'complex' selling second-hand clothes and doilies later make an appearance at the match as the paramedics.

Thoroughly depressed we head back to the hotel. The players are very relaxed as they watch Auckland scrape a victory against the Waratahs (mainly due to a knock-on that only ref Jonathan Kaplan saw).

On the way to the match there is a large billboard at an intersection near the ground advertising a match between the Bulldogs and Eagles, with 'Sharks vs Hurricanes' an after-thought in small type underneath. An omen of sorts perhaps.

The press box/hutch is a rather tatty park bench that only serves to emphasise the uncomfortableness of the match that follows. Just behind me former Sharks hooker John Allan makes his Supersport commentating debut.

The Sharks start well enough, other than a shocking penalty attempt from Honiball, and get the first try when Stephen Brink follows up and falls on yet another flawless André Joubert grubber.

Early on Wellington really don't seem capable of winning — they infringe constantly and even Christian Cullen knocks on twice when under no pressure. The Sharks keep up the pressure and really should have wrapped up the game by half-time.

The Sharks attack from a lineout exploiting space in the centres but Gillingham passes left with Fyvie to his right and the line open. The ball goes to no-one and with that the game slips away.

Van Rensburg is isolated, the Hurricanes exploit the tackle ball law and Umaga is off down the line exchanging passes with Holwell before going over himself.

Worse is to follow as Juba counter-attacks, Telea blocks the chip and off-loads to Cullen who casually sidesteps a lock and two props before strolling over. The Hurricanes race into a 15 point lead and there is a look of shock on Sharks faces.

Their spirits can't have been lifted by the stadium announcer constantly playing the Hurricanes theme tune, which to top it all, is awful. This makes an absolute mockery of the fixture being a home game and clearly irritates the players.

After half-time the Sharks work hard to stay in contention and Hentie Martens goes over.

Crucially they lose momentum when they elect to kick for posts instead of for position late in the half. The ball wobbles wide and the Hurricanes are able to relieve the pressure. A scintillating burst down the line from replacement Justin Swart nearly leads to a try but the ball is turned over again.
A late try under the posts ensures that the Sharks are unable to gain even a consolation point by staying within seven points. They walk off exhausted and spirits only lift on the flight home as we celebrate John Smit's 21st birthday.]

Previous Page, from left: *John Smit, Chris Rossouw and Ollie Le Roux get ready to pack down*
Above: *Henry Honiball gets a pass away before he can be tackled by Christian Cullen.*
Below: *Don't tell us how hard you work. Physio Dave Becker takes a break as Ollie Le Roux and Warren Brosnihan massage Stephen Brink before the game.*
Opposite: *Hentie Martens goes airborne as he clears from the back of a ruck.*

BMW
Ford
Reebok

vs Stormers

***The Sharks 19 vs Western Stormers 35**, Norwich Park Newlands, Cape Town, April 11*

***Sharks:** Joubert, Brink, Payne, Muller, Swart, Honiball, Martens, Teichmann, Fyvie, Andrews, Slade, van Rensburg, Smit, Rossouw, Le Roux*

***Stormers:** Montgomery, Paulse, Fleck, Marinos, Rossouw, van Straaten, van Zyl, Skinstad, Brink, Trytsman, Boome, Krige, Visagie, Marais, Kempson*

The game that everyone was looking forward to. The Stormers are in scintillating form and apart from throwing a game against Otago have looked mightily impressive.

Naas Botha described it earlier in the week as the game of the season, which it certainly is from a South African point of view. It is intriguing in terms of the personal battles within the wider context of the game. Joubert vs Montgomery, Muller vs Fleck, Honiball vs Van Straaten and the big one, Teichmann vs Skinstad. There is also the matter of the stolen kit. In a desperate attempt to get an image and some support the Stormers have decided that black would be a unique colour for them to wear — unique if you've never in your life seen a Sharks game. Sharks CEO, Brian van Zyl, says he nearly choked on his drink when he saw the black kit unveiled at the official launch of the Super 12.

It seems a small matter but it has stoked the fires of a rivalry which has grown fairly intense over the past couple of seasons. Newlands has a reputation for giving the opposition a hostile reception and I found it particularly unpleasant on this occasion. The press box itself is only half-full of journalists, the rest of the space is taken up by wives, girlfriends and sundry other Stormers 'faithful.'

The Sharks start well and get the first try of the game when Charl van Rensburg goes over after a back-row move in which Gary Teichmann is prominent. However they are unable to make their possession count and the boot of Braam van Straaten and a Breyton Paulse try bring the Stormers back into contention.

While the Sharks are competitive up-front they can't match the creative flair of the Stormers back three: Paulse, Rossouw and Montgomery who are all playing with a great

15

deal of confidence.
There is a bit of controversy when referee Tappe Henning ignores the half-time hooter in preference to his own stop-watch. This incenses Stormers captain Bobby Skinstad who comes disturbingly close to throwing a tantrum.
Just after half-time a cleverly worked quick lineout between Paulse and Rossouw sees the latter over in the corner for a try which van Straaten converts to push the lead to 20-8.
The Sharks dominate the next 20 minutes through the relentless driving of the forwards which results in a try in the corner from Justin Swart and another Honiball penalty. At 20-16 the Sharks are still in with a shout but it is the game-breaking skills of Rossouw and Skinstad which make the difference. In quick succession flowing back-line moves result in tries from Anton Leonard and Breyton Paulse.
At the press conference afterwards Gary Teichmann, for perhaps the first time ever, comes close to losing his temper. The gloriously inept Grant Robbins of *Sportsday* puts it to Gary that he and his forwards were played off the park by younger more hungry men. With a withering stare Gary delivers his reply : "I don't know which game you were watching but I think you'll find that it is one area of the game that we dominated."
Mac is as magnanimous as ever: "We lost to a better team on the day. We can have no complaints." With that it is back to Durban. Hopes of a semi-final are now in some doubt with only one home game left.]

Previous Page
Left: *Chris Rossouw moments before he puts the man outside him, Justin Swart, into the corner.*
Right: *Henry Honiball attempts to charge down a Percy Montgomery clearance.*

Top: *A section of the 50 000 crowd.*
Bottom: *One of the 'men in black' gets his two inches of fame, much to the bemusement of Justin Swart.*
Right: *Breyton Paulse (left) and Stormers captain Bobby Skinstad celebrate after Paulse's second decisive try of the game.*
Opposite: *Morné vd Merwe, Nico Wegner, Chad Alcock and Joe Gillingham watch glumly as the Sharks get beaten for the second week in a row.*

SENTRASURE
aska
FEDSURE
GOEIE HOOP FM
SYFIN
PRICE FORBES
VOICE MAIL
PHILIPS PHILIPS PHILIPS
MURRAY & ROBERTS
FEDSURE FEDS

vs Bulls

***The Sharks 29 vs Northern Bulls 0**, The Stadium Kings Park, Durban, 17 April*

***Sharks:** Swart, Terblanche, Kayser, Muller, Brink, Honiball, Martens, Teichmann, Fyvie, Andrews, Atherton, Brosnihan, Moyle, Rossouw, Le Roux*

***Northern Bulls:** Goosen, Welsh, Esterhuizen, Julies, Olivier, Smith, De Kock, Brand, Bekker, vd Walt, Otto, Basson, Espag, vd Walt D, Ribbens*

The Bulls arrive at Kings Park in woeful form made worse by an impossibly long injury list. Intense media pressure has focused on the coaching abilities of Eugene Van Wyk, one of the nicest men in South African rugby, seemingly disregarding the fact that he was a Currie Cup winning coach only six months earlier.

The Sharks are expected to win comfortably but it's a trap that Mac is determined his team won't fall into. Flanker Charl van Rensburg is rested, Brent Moyle returns for John Smit and Deon Kayser makes his first start at outside centre.

The Sharks start well and never really look like losing their grip on the game as their forwards dominate. The first half follows a predictable pattern and while the Bulls are game and competitive they cannot make any real impression on the Sharks.

Henry Honiball kicks four penalties before Justin Swart crosses the line just before half time. The need for a bonus point is pressing and the crowd, judging by the number of attempted Mexican Waves is getting restless. The powerful motivating effect of aimlessly throwing your hands in the air is rewarded when two further tries are added through Terblanche and Kayser.

Despite almost constant pressure the Sharks are unable to get the crucial fourth try. Twice they go over the line only to be called back for infringements by referee Andy Turner and on countless occasions they simply take the wrong option.

More worrying is an injury to captain Gary Teichmann. He leaves the field at the end of the first half with a knee ligament problem. It is almost certain that he won't be on the plane to Australia tomorrow but Mac refuses to reveal anything: "We'll see what the medical people say and then make a decision," is all you can get out of him.

So it's off to Australia the next day without the captain, with only one of the expected crop of bonus points and four extremely tough matches looming.]

***Below:** Teichmann in action before he is forced to leave the field with a knee ligament problem.*
***Right:** Deon Kayser bursts through to score.*
***Following page:** The replacements warm-down after the game.*

GILBER
anon

RUGBY

Australasia

The itinerary for the next month looks quite straightforward. Durban to Johannesburg to Sydney to Auckland. Play the Auckland Blues. To Taupo to Hamilton. Play the Waikato Chiefs. To Christchurch to Queenstown back to Christchurch. Play the Canterbury Crusaders. To Brisbane. Play the Queensland Reds. Contest a semi-final or go straight home.

Mac is looking very chipper as he gets on the plane for Sydney despite the criticism the team received in the Sunday newspapers. Just briefly it feels as if we are off on holiday, leaving our cares behind.

After promising to follow the teams anti-jet lag routine of fresh fruit, lots of water and no alcohol we crumble within an hour of leaving. The food is surprisingly good and it seems rude not to have a bit of wine too.

Sydney is wild and windy and recovering from a hail storm which has caused millions of dollars of damage. The only excitement is caused by a bit of over-zealous frisking from a customs officer as the Australian authorities fight the good fight to prevent rogue seeds and biltong from devastating the continent.

Sydney is awash with Olympic 2000 souvenirs and hundreds of construction sights. The traffic is a nightmare but it is still one of the most beautiful cities in the world. After a day or two of sight-seeing we head off on a three hour flight to Auckland.

The team are incredulous as they are met with bright sunshine. Juba remarks that's it's the first time he has landed in New Zealand and he hasn't been met by wind and rain. And this is about his sixth visit.

Auckland markets itself as the city of sails, as apparently one in five people own a boat of some sort. There is water on either side of this beautiful city which blends comfortably into the surrounding hills. Auckland is also preparing for New Zealand's defence of the America's Cup in 2000 so the yacht theme is everywhere.]

vs Blues

***The Sharks 12 vs Auckland Blues 6**, Eden Park, Auckland, 24 April*
***Sharks**: Joubert, Swart, Kayser, Gillingham, Terblanche, Honiball, Martens, Andrews, Fyvie, van Rensburg, Atherton, Wegner, Le Roux, Rossouw, Smit*
***Blues:** Cashmore, Vidiri, Innes, Lowen, Howlett, Spencer, Robinson, Jones, Carter, Taylor, Brooke, Reichelmann, Barrel, McFarland, Coughlan*

At the airport I'm stopped by a customs official who only seems interested in Bobby Skinstad's car accident, but the news has passed me by in jet-lag limbo so I can't offer any enlightenment.
The Cats are also in town and there is plenty of interest in both teams. The senior players are well-respected as is Mac, whom the Kiwi's don't expect to see again in a coaching capacity.
It couldn't last. Match day Saturday and the rain has arrived and it falls pretty constantly. That afternoon the Cats contrived to throw away a comfortable lead and hand victory to The Chiefs. Sunday Times rugby writer, Dan Retief, nearly chokes on his beer as Boeta Wessels misses a simple touch and hands victory to The Chiefs.

> **"Don't ask me how bad they were, lets talk about how good we were,"**
> *Mac*

The Sharks have never won at Eden Park, in fact no touring side has won there since the Naas Botha-inspired Springboks of 1981. The press box has the best food we've tasted in a rugby stadium so far this season, and in keeping with the general impression of New Zealanders gained so far, the staff and local journalists are very friendly.
Mac springs a few surprises with his pack selection. Three locks start with Warren Brosnihan on the bench. The match pattern soon settles into one of siege as the Blues batter away at the Sharks line. It is reminiscent of old-style rugby — not pretty to watch but hugely enjoyable for both sets of forwards. The ploy of using an extra lock is soon abandoned and Warren Brosnihan is on the pitch before half-time.
Mac moves constantly between the touchline and his seat in the stand. It's not just nerves but a ploy to avoid the TV cameras. His pitch-side antics and intense, pained expressions have earned him the nickname 'serial killer' and an anguished Mac expression is a favourite with the local TV producer.
Blues full-back Adrian Cashmore is normally deadly with the boot but not tonight. Henry Honiball meanwhile is on form and succeeds with his first kick. Justin Swart is then sin-binned for blatant obstruction on Joeli Vidiri. That it happened outside the 22 rules out the possibility of a penalty try. Cashmore converts the resulting penalty and the Sharks begin to creak.
The Blues apply continual pressure but the 14 men survive a series of six scrums on their line. Exasperated the Blues take a penalty kick which Cashmore misses.
A torrential downpour greets the players as they come out for the second-half. It makes handling difficult and the game remains dour. There is a brief moment of excitement as Stefan Terblanche breaks clear but he ignores the man outside him and the chance goes begging.
In response to the state of the game or more probably the creative paucity of the Blues performance the attention of the journalists begins to wander. Golf courses around the rugby playing world are discussed and the common consensus is that André Joubert is perhaps the world's best golfing rugby player.
On the field the Blues still can't break down the Sharks and two more Honiball penalties edge the Sharks out to a 12-3 lead. To their credit the Blues continue to throw the ball

Previous page: *Chris Rossouw (centre) tries to maul his way forward with the help of Wayne Fyvie (right)*
Above: *The thin black line - Atherton and Martens close down Carlos Spencer.*
Below left: *A familiar sight to Sharks fans - Mark Andrews replacing a contact lens during the game.*
Below right: *Deon Kayser can't stop wing Joeli Vidiri from getting his pass away.*

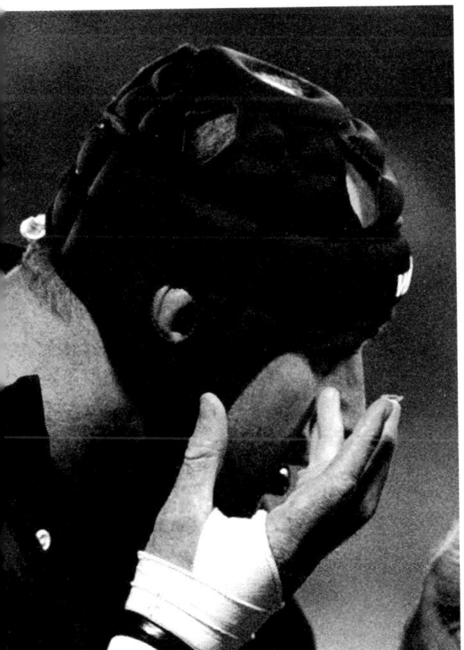

around but resolute defence continually forces them into handling errors.

At the final whistle the elation of the Sharks is apparent. They have been on the end of a couple of beatings at Eden Park so this win is really special. The press conference contains some vintage Mac. Asked if he thought the Blues were poor he replies: "Don't ask me how bad they were, lets talk about how good we were," with a big smile on his face.

The win lifts the Sharks back into semi-final contention and also confounds many sceptics who doubted they had the depth to sustain a challenge.

The after-match function is held in the Blues change-room with only the players and team management invited. After the way they have been knocking lumps out of each other on the field it is quite an eye-opener to see the warmth and genuine friendliness between the players. It certainly makes a mockery of the assumption that the professional age has taken all the heart, spirit and camaraderie from the game. Robin Brooke is kind enough to suggest a suitable pub, the Carlton, for a little light after-match celebration and tells us that the Cats 'did alright there last week,' whatever that means?

As we leave the ground nearly an hour-and-a-half afterwards there is still a small band of South Africans standing in the rain waving flags, waiting to meet their heroes and speak a little Afrikaans. All of the players make an effort to greet them. "Dankie, dat julle gekom," says Ollie Le Roux, "dankie vir die support." *(Thank you for coming, thanks for the support.)*

The Crusaders scrape a victory against the Bulls through the drop-kicking and gesturing of Andrew Mehrtens. This increases the jam at the top of the table but the Sharks leave Auckland full of optimism, and the odd hangover.]

From top:

Justin Swart, Stefan Terblanche and Hentie Martens full of smiles after the game;

Well played master! Mac congratulates André Joubert;

Equally chuffed is Hugh Reece-Edwards, giving scrum-half Martens a big hug of appreciation;

Lock Steve Atherton gives his boots a wash in the shower after the game. We never did find out how he got them dry in time for the next game.

Opposite:

Each game about a mile of Elastoplast goes into making sure that Wayne Fyvie's knee stays together. He badly injured it two seasons ago and through sheer self-belief has managed to continue his career.

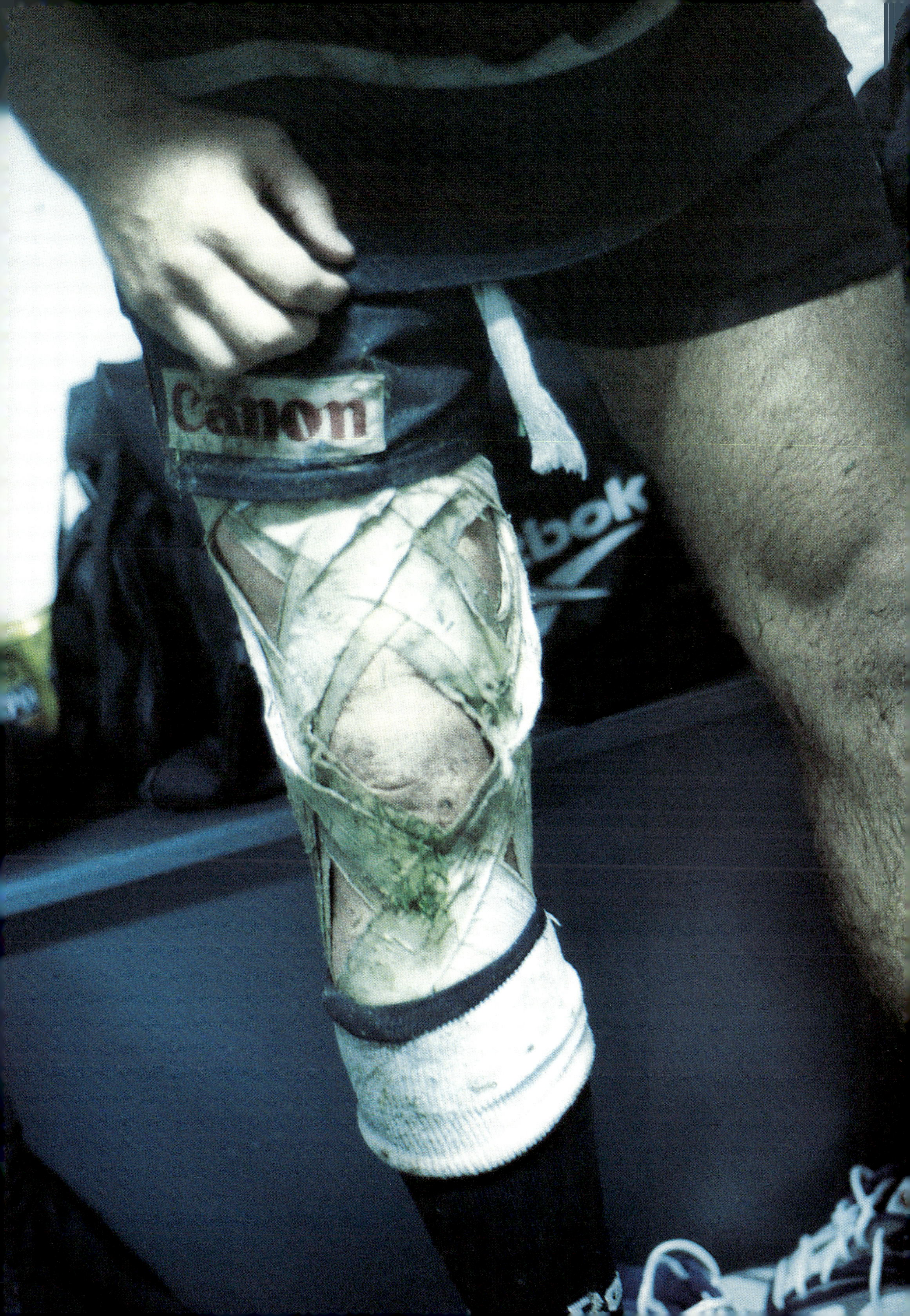
Canon

Reebok
SHARKS
Reebok

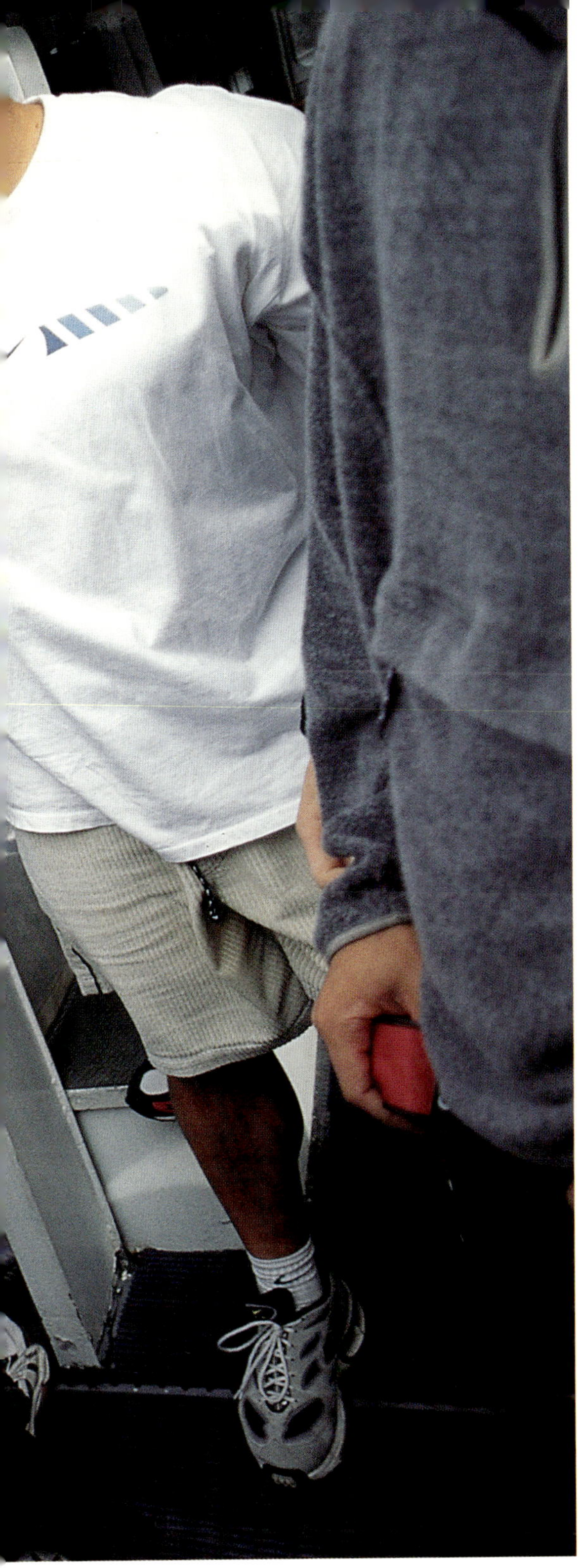

Taupo

Taupo

Very, very, very early the next morning the team get on the bus to Taupo, a couple of hours south of Auckland. Taupo sits glumly on the largest natural lake in the southern hemisphere, I think. The lake is a result of an explosion/meteorite strike thousands of years ago.

Taupo is a haven for thrill seeking backpackers looking to bungy-jump, sky-dive and indulge in similar other adrenaline-raising sports so beloved of New Zealanders. Unfortunately none of these pursuits are open to the players so they have to settle for golf and fishing.

Chad Alcock is a famous fisherman, at least in the Eastern Cape, and amid much hype and fanfare takes to the water. To great hilarity he catches nothing, not even a bite. The players while away their time with a trip on the lake, nobody catches a thing, and plenty of sleeping.

The euphoria of the weekend's victory fades somewhat as the injury list is revealed. Honiball has a stiff neck, Joubert a sore knee, Muller is still not quite ready and everyone else is generally aching. Although Mac doesn't reveal it at the time he remarks that, "the change room looked like a battlefield." Physio Steve Felsher is booked from morning till midnight all week.

The team train in the evening at the Taupo Rugby Club. We are all bundled up against the cold but, providing an eerie insight into why Kiwi rugby players are so hard, a group of small children run around barefoot and slide across the dewy grass.

A special point is made of thanking the Taupo rugby club for their help and hospitality. "Even when I was here with the Springboks we used to get given inferior facilities, but these guys, who are under no obligation to help us, have gone out of their way to make us feel welcome. Thank you." says Mac.]

Above: *The picture women all over South Africa have been waiting years for. Ollie le Roux reveals André Joubert's hidden assets.*

Left: *Happy campers. Henry Honiball and Hentie Martens really start to miss home.*

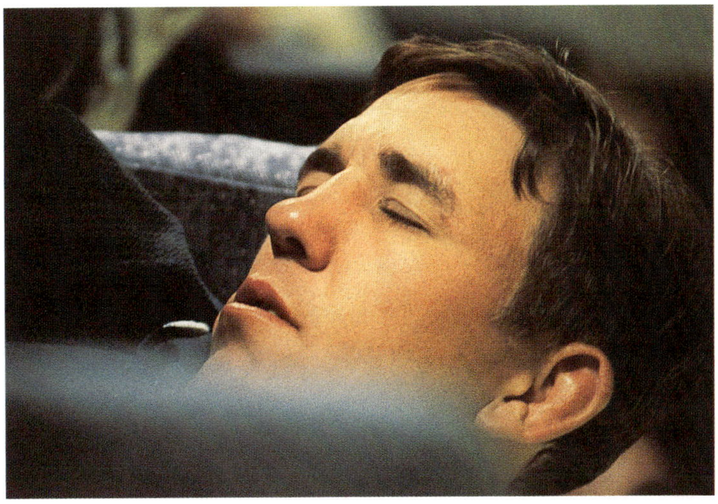

Sleeping beauties. Rugby is hard work. Touring and travelling is even harder.

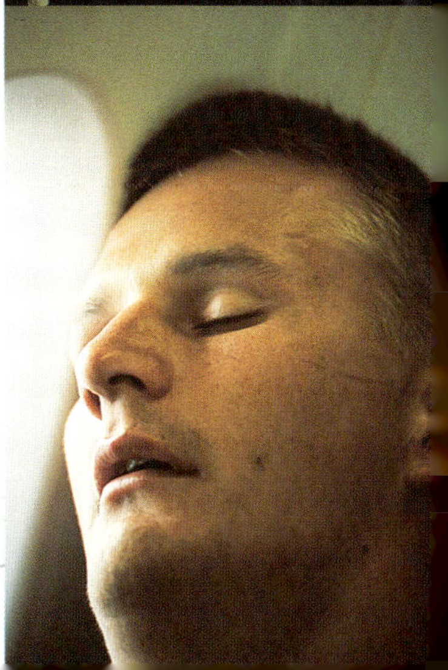

31

Hamilton

Hamilton

Hamilton is the hub at the centre of one of New Zealand's most prolific farming districts, King Country. A quiet flat town it is bucolic and friendly in the extreme.

It's main claim to fame is the giant agricultural fair held in June and, as far as South Africans are concerned, the venue of the infamous 'cancelled' game during the Boks 1981 tour.

As a pointer to the depth of feeling for rugby in New Zealand one need look no further than the local daily paper The Waikato Times. On a Thursday it carries a ten page supplement dealing exclusively with local club rugby. Something a city the size of Durban can't manage where our journalists are lucky if they get the space for 500 words on the provincial side, let alone the clubs. Morné van der Merwe arrives after an epic journey as front row cover for Brent Moyle. Brent who has acquired the nickname, The Tourist, has been unable to train due to a stud pressure sore which has turned septic.

The weather is still mild and the sun fairly beats down — the players keep looking to the sky to see if the rain is coming.]

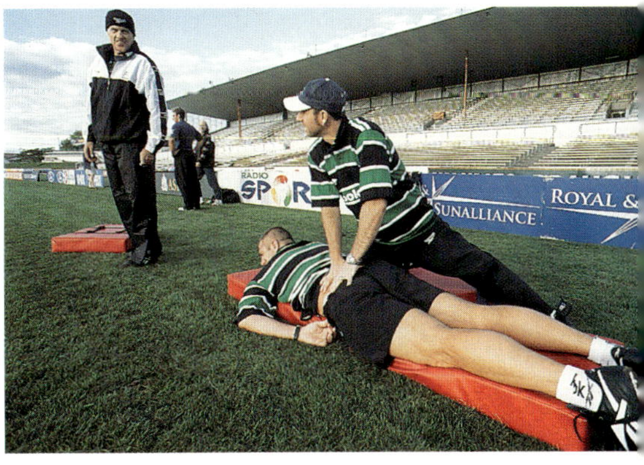

Left: *Something you didn't ever think you would see. Mark Andrews and Steve Atherton soak up the rays at the team motel in Hamilton.*

From top: *Physio Steve Felsher and doctor Glen Hagemann watch as Mac puts the team through their paces;*

The game against the Blues was so hard that Hugh Reece-Edwards got sore just watching. Steve Felsher gives him a rub down much to Mac's amusement;

Team barber/hair stylist Hentie Martens gives John Slade a short back and sides to help him move faster through the air;

Shaun Payne practices his throwing in. Luckily the injury crisis isn't so bad that he'll be pressed into front-row duty.

vs Chiefs

***The Sharks 19 vs Waikato Chiefs 32**, Rugby Park, Hamilton, 30 April*
***Sharks:** Swart, Terblanche, Kayser, Gillingham, Payne, Benadé, Alcock, Brosnihan, Fyvie, Andrews, Atherton, van Rensburg, Fynn, Visser, Le Roux*
***Chiefs:** Reihana, Randle, McLeod, Little, Lomu, Jackson, Duggan, Mika, Marsh, Davis, Jones, Holten, Martin, Smith, Lidgard*

Ditto last week — as soon as the players start packing their kit the rain starts coming down, and it doesn't stop.
Mac decides to rest Pieter Muller and Hentie Martens and is deprived through injury of André Joubert and Henry Honiball. The continuing absence through injury of Brad McLeod-Henderson, sore groin, and Brent Moyle also limits his options. Etienne Fynn makes his Super 12 debut as John Smit is given a rest on the bench.
After the game there is much talk back in Durban that Mac had put out a second string side which I think is more than a little harsh. On the night they are out-played by a very good, but until now under-achieving, Waikato side.
The Chiefs come into the game with their confidence boosted by their last gasp win against the Cats and obviously keen to enjoy their last home game. It is also the game when Jonah Lomu decides to shake off the cobwebs and get fully involved for the first time in a couple of years. And how he gets involved.
The Chiefs supporters turn up in good numbers despite the weather to say farewell to their team. Waikato fans are in the habit of bringing cow bells and duck calls to the game which makes a change from another tedious chorus of 'Olé, Olé, Olé.'
The Sharks don't play well. In the first half they fail to use the wind to keep the Chiefs pinned back and their option taking is poor. Credit must also go to a hugely committed Chiefs side. With it taking three people to stop Lomu the centre pairing of Little and McLeod capitalise on the space this creates.
Chad Alcock scores twice for the Sharks but one can't help feeling that many of the Sharks difficulties

came at half-back where the wrong option is taken too often.
They are unable to capitalise on the sending-off just before half-time of Chiefs skipper Dylan Mika for a vicious head high tackle on Shaun Payne. John Smit on early for Etienne Fynn is then sent to the sin-bin for a needless bit of rucking which is followed up with a punch.
At the heart of everything for the Chiefs is Lomu. Like a slim-line combine harvester churning up defenders he makes space that wing Roger Randle exploits to grab a couple of tries. The moment that defines it all is when Lomu picks up Justin Swart and slams him into the ground. I think it's how many of the Sharks felt.
The Chiefs convert the chances that come their way while the Sharks squander a number of chances and don't utilise the amount of possession they have. Once again they fail to register a bonus point.
Afterwards there was a sombre mood in the camp with captain Wayne Fyvie even going so far as to suggest that the team hadn't been committed enough. There are also dark mutterings about the performance of referee Stuart Dickinson. Ross Cooper, coach of the Chiefs, believes it is one of his sides best ever performances while Mac simply says, "they were more passionate, they wanted it more."
Fly-half Jacques Benadé confides in us that he is never going to let his children play rugby if there are guys like Lomu around. He has borne the brunt of Lomu's charging runs from the blindside wing and it wasn't fun.]

Previous page: *Jonah Lomu at the bottom of the pile of bodies it took to stop him.*

Opposite page:

Top: *Mornay Visser makes his long run for freedom. They caught him.*

Bottom from left:

Captain Wayne Fyvie seeks clarification from referee Stuart Dickinson, again;

Etienne Fynn makes a fraught Super 12 debut against the Chiefs;

The slightly crazed and manic Chiefs support;

Jacques Benadé, in for the injured Henry Honiball, prepares himself for yet another Chiefs attack spearheaded by a resurgent Jonah Lomu.

Queenstown

The morning after the Chiefs game, tired and slightly bedraggled, we fly to Queenstown, the country's 'real' adventure capital on New Zealand's South Island. Popular with touring teams it is also the place where the All Blacks go to let off a bit of steam.

Queenstown is a stunningly picturesque town. It nestles next to Lake Wakatipu in the shadow of snow capped mountains. It's Mac's favourite place in New Zealand and it has become a regular stop during the past couple of seasons.

There isn't as much relaxing as planned after the Chiefs result. Everyone is disappointed with the performance. Mac holds a couple of 'old-fashioned' training sessions. Drop the ball and you run around the posts and whatever you do don't come last.

The players manage to sneak out to sample some of the adventures on offer. A luge ride ends in a spectacular crash and a couple of bruises and limps have to be hidden from Mac. Warren Brosnihan, Mike Greenaway, Glen Hagemann and Sean take a ride on the 'fly-by-wire.' The flying machine/cage is in a gorge. It is winched backwards until you are at a 90º angle. You then press a release button and swoop down into the gorge at a stomach churning speed. Everyone survives.]

Left: *The lake as seen from the Skyline restaurant.*
Bottom left to right:
Two views of Queenstown;
The players take a breather during training;
Cards, always cards;
Allister Coetzee and Dr Glen Hagemann watch as Mac puts the players through their paces;
The magnificent man in his flying machine. Warren Brosnihan hurtles through the air at 170 km/h on the 'fly-by-wire.'

vs Crusaders

The Sharks 29 vs Canterbury Crusaders 34,
Lancaster park, Christchurch, May 8
Sharks: *Swart, Terblanche, Kayser, Muller, Brink, Honiball, Martens, Brosnihan, Fyvie, Andrews, Atherton, Van Rensburg, Smit, Rossouw, Le Roux*
Crusaders: *MacDonald, So'oalo, Berryman, Gibson, Ralph, Mehrtens, Marshall, McLeod, Robertson, Maxwell, Blackadder, Thorne, Somerville, Hammett, Feek*

The Sharks arrived in Christchurch on the Thursday before the game unashamedly looking to settle some scores. Last season they blew their chances of a Super 12 home semi-final by losing to the Crusaders at home. They then gave the Crusaders a 20 point start at Lancaster Park before clawing themselves back into the game with only the sin-binning of Boeta Wessels costing them a deserved victory. The Crusaders then went on to beat the Auckland Blues and claim their first title.

In a similar vein to last season the Crusaders are running into form at just the right time. After scraping victory in Pretoria against the Bulls they found themselves 31-6 down against the Cats yet came back to win 58-36. Unfortunately for the Sharks it is the second week in a row that they will be playing opponents who have received a huge confidence boost after victories over the Cats.

After the intensity of training in Queenstown the team are keyed up and confident. Henry Honiball returns as does Pieter Muller while the pack is at full strength. A chilly night in Christchurch plays host to one of the most compelling matches of the tournament so far.

In the first-half the Sharks play with a fervour and intensity that later led Mac to describe it as "probably the best 40 minutes this side has ever played." The tight five turn in a towering display with Ollie Le Roux at the forefront of everything.

After 14 minutes he fields a kick near the half-way line and begins to charge. He exchanges passes with Brosnihan before sending Pieter Muller in for his first try. He is then prominent in setting up Stefan Terblanche to go over in the corner 11 minutes later.

With a minute of the half remaining Warren Brosnihan picks up at the base of the scrum and brushes off a couple of tacklers before going over under the posts, 22-6.

Despite this score the 10 minutes either side of half-time proves critical. Firstly the engine room is decimated when Mark Andrews goes off with an ankle injury and Steve Atherton breaks his hand.

> *"they couldn't lay a hand on us Bros"*
>
> *Ollie Le Roux relives Pieter Muller's first try*

Worse is to follow with the news that Henry Honiball has damaged ligaments in his ankle. Being Henry, he has it strapped up and goes back onto the field. The medical staff pleaded with him not to go back on but he insists. Months later they were still incredulous that anyone could play through that much pain.

These injuries give the Crusaders the fillip they need and, in the case of Honiball, vital time and space for his opposite number Andrew Mehrtens. So'oalo makes the break-through when he out-wits and out-muscles Stephen Brink to score in the corner.

Chris Rossouw is then sin-binned for a late charge and while he is off the field Caleb Ralph and Mehrtens added converted tries. Within 15 minutes of the re-start the score is 31-22 and the Sharks are forced into playing desperate catch-up rugby.

Pieter Muller scores his second try close to the posts after a tapped penalty to bring the Sharks within two points but Mehrtens stretches the lead once more with his fourth penalty of the evening.

Disconsolate is not a strong enough word to

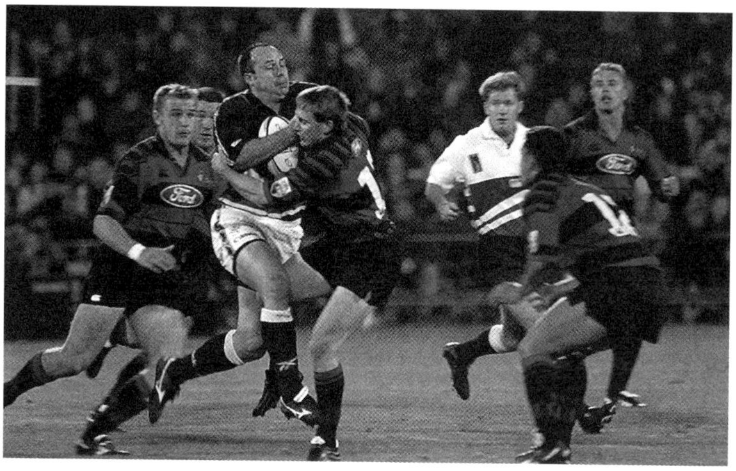

Above: *Pieter Muller charges into Andrew Mehrtens.*
Below: *Charl van Rensburg and Steve Atherton get ready to contest a lineout.*
Opposite: *Warren Brosnihan carries on a move started by Ollie Le Roux that leads to the first try of the game for centre Pieter Muller.*

describe the feeling in the dressing room after the game. The players look shattered, unwilling to believe that they have lost. Home has never seemed further away than it does that evening.

Amazingly the Sharks still have an outside chance of a semi-final berth. Despite this it is a battered and bruised side that make their way back across the Tasman Sea for the final game against the Queensland Reds.]

Below left: *Chris Rossouw and his parents look at pictures of his new-born son at a cyber café in Christchurch. The Rossouws followed their son around New Zealand and Australia in a camper van.*
Below right: *While waiting for the bus to leave Chad Alcock and Warren Brosnihan still find time for one more game of one-bounce.*
Opposite: *Things go awry at Lancaster Park as a Kiwi tries to get a braai going.*

PHILIPS
Smiths City
PHILIPS
Smiths City
PlayStation.
McDonald's
Telecom
AIR NEW ZEALAND
TOWER
TOWER
The National Bank
The National Bank

LIFEGUARD

vs Reds

The Sharks 13 vs 34 Queensland Reds, *Ballymore, Brisbane, 14 May*
The Sharks: *Joubert, Terblanche, Payne, Muller, Swart, Benade, Alcock, Brosnihan, Fyvie, Wegner, Slade, van Rensburg, Smit, Rossouw, Le Roux*
Queensland Reds: *Latham, Tune, Herbert, Horan, Smith, Spooner, Raulini, Kefu, Murray, Connors, Waugh, Cockbain, Panoho, Foley, Crowley*

The Sharks arrive in Brisbane on Australia's Gold Coast sad and sore. Four players, Moyle, Andrews, Atherton and Honiball have gone home while promising Under 21's Piet Myburgh and Butch James join the squad.

The week before the game is somewhat flat after the disappointment of Christchurch. There is a lot of time to kill and after a month away everyone is very keen to get home. There is not as much focus on the team as there was in New Zealand and so there is less pressure.

The Sharks have an outside chance of qualifying for the semis, more a mathematical probability than anything concrete. While they focus on the game one gets the feeling that more thoughts are with home. Golf, trips to the theme park, Movie World, and plenty of shopping dominate the week.

It seems that lingerie is the gift of choice. After a tentative initial purchase from one of the more experienced players the next couple of days sees a stream of players frequenting the same shop. "If only Australian men were as romantic and thoughtful as you guys," remarked the sales assistant. If only she knew.

Australia is a very safety conscious country, obsessively so some would perhaps say. The lifeguard on the previous page is standing watch over a pond — no more than waist deep — next to the river that runs through Brisbane. Top job.

Other highlights were Sean comprehensively beating André Joubert at pool, perhaps the word hustled

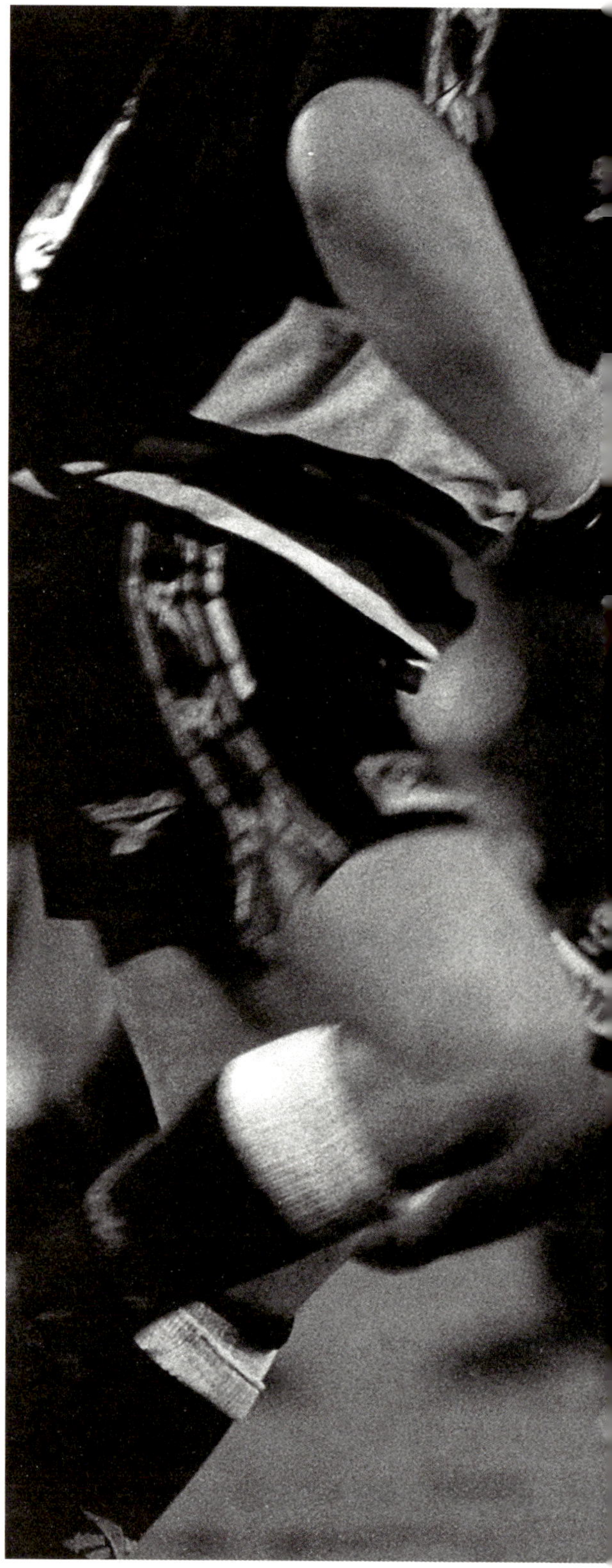

Above: *Chad Alcock clears from a ruck.*
From left:
Old rivals Tim Horan and Ollie Le Roux; Anthony Fani, Butch James and an over-excited Etienne Fynn before the game; Piet 'Spud' Myburgh is chuffed with his first Super 12 appearance.

SLADE
5

110
109

would be more appropriate but that would lessen the glory of Seans' triumph. A memory he will no doubt carry to the grave.

The Reds are assured of a semi-final spot and are looking for a bonus point to ensure they get a game at home. Their side is full of Australian internationals, particularly in the back-line and the Sharks will have their work cut-out.

Much like the week before The Sharks dominate the first-half and go in 8-7 ahead through a Benadé penalty and a Shaun Payne try. And again, much like the week before their opponents save their best for the second-half. Wallaby centre Daniel Herbert scores twice and further scores from Brett Johnstone and Mark Connors ensure the bonus point.

The Sharks in keeping with their performances throughout the tournament don't play badly and are always competitive but they just can't get the points on the board. They look tired in the second-half with their thoughts already on the flight home.

Despite the performance Mac is not too downcast; "We're obviously disappointed after such a promising first-half performance. I'm very proud of the way we played considering that its been a long four weeks and the number of injuries we've had."

The team have two days to kill after the game so they let their hair down a little. Just a little, before its back to Durban to start preparing for the start of the Currie Cup.]

***From top*:**

Team Director Mike Kelroe-Cooke practices his putting in the foyer of the hotel;

Journalist Mike Greenaway and Allister Coetzee absorb a couple of blows as Stefan Terblanche loosens up his shoulders;

Piet, Butch, John and Brad waiting for the flight;

Ollie Le Roux does some pre-game stretching.

Next Page: *Some of the team at the function after the game. From left back row: Warren Brosnihan, Deon Kayser, Joe Gillingham, Shaun Payne, Morné vd Merwe, Chris Rossouw, Allister Coetzee, John Smit, Kevin Stevenson, Jacques Benadé, Glen Hagemann, Nico Wegner, Steve Felsher, Butch James.*

Front: Chad Alcock, Pieter Muller, Hentie Martens and Piet Myburgh.

Right: *Chad Alcock and Morné vd Merwe enjoying one of the rides at Movie World.*
Below: *I love you too. Morné vd Merwe calls home before boarding the plane.*

Reebok
Reebok

vodacom
vodacom
vodacom
Canon

Training

The one area that has changed the most, indeed been revolutionised since the introduction of professionalism, is fitness training. The players obviously have more time to dedicate to fitness and as such are in brilliant shape.

The aim of the training can basically be divided into two categories. Pre and early season training is aimed at getting each player into 'rugby-shape,' giving them the endurance to get around the field. Most of the players maintain this level of fitness throughout the year.

During the season a lot of emphasis is placed on developing explosiveness — which gives the player ability to break tackles, take half-gaps and exploit space. In the modern game coaches look to this explosiveness to create 'patterns of play' around.

Explosive power is honed in a variety of ways; in the gym, 'spin classes,' and in specialised routines devised by fitness advisers Kevin Stevenson and Barry Angus.

Spin classes are the latest exercise trend. Everyone is on an exercise bike and an instructor leads them through a series of gradients and speeds. Spinning comes closest to replicating the varying degrees of exertion and movement during actual match conditions.

A particular favourite of Barry is the sprint up 50 steps on the extremely steep gradient of the upper tier of the East Stand. Players who are at similar fitness levels are grouped together. The leader of each group wears a cardio-monitor. Each group sprints up the steps and then takes a slow walk down.

By the time they have reached the bottom their heart rates should have decreased or stabilised at 160 beats per minute. The moment it stabilises they sprint up again. Gradually the heart begins to hit 200 beats-per-minute and takes longer to return to 160. The premium zone for explosive exercise is when the heart stays between 160 and 180.

Flank Charl Van Rensburg usually puts in the best performance at this exercise as his heart rate stabilises faster than anyone else. Fitness Adviser Barry Angus describes him as having a huge engine.

The benefits of this sort of exercise began to make themselves plain during the season. The strength that Trevor Halstead has gained has pushed up his performance levels markedly and given him a great deal of confidence. His ability to break through tackles and take the half-gap has resulted in a number of tries.]

Left: *An impressive backdrop to the dreaded step exercises.*

Above: *Hooker Chris Pearson practices his throwing in.*

Next Page: *Etienne Fynn and Brad McCleod-Henderson strike a pose in the gym.*

Reebok

Reebok

From top:

Parachute running on tour in Hamilton;

Charl van Rensburg and Rex Elliott taking strain during a spin class at the Kings Park Health & Racquet;

Justin Swart at full tilt during training.

Right: *Ollie Le Roux during a work-out at the gym.*

Overleaf: *Tackling practice in Hamilton.*

WAIKATO DRAUGHT
WAIKATO DRAUGHT

Konica

Reebok
Canon
Canon
Canon
Bankfin

vs Falcons

vs Falcons

The Sharks 17 vs Gauteng Falcons 12, *The Stadium, Kings Park, Durban, 11 June*
Sharks: *Bennett, Welsh, Payne, Gillingham, Swart, vd Westhuyzen, Martens, Brosnihan, Fyvie, van Rensburg, Slade, Wegner, Moyle, Rossouw, Smit*
Falcons: *Du Toit, Matthys, Lourens, Meyer, van Deventer, van As, De Kock, Rossouw, Koloi, Boardman, Schroeder, Booysen, Espag, vd Walt, Williamson*

With obscene haste after the end of the Super 12 the premier South African provincial competition, the Currie Cup, starts for the Sharks with a lethargic and indifferent performance.

The Falcons will look back on this game knowing it was a golden opportunity to get their campaign off to a winning start yet they are unable to transmit their enthusiasm, and The Sharks' indifference, into points.

Joubert, Teichmann and Garvey all start on the bench. Brent Moyle gets his first Natal cap against his old team-mates and Under 21 stars Frikkie Welsh and Jaco van der Westhuyzen are drafted in.

After going behind to a Piet Matthys try, the Sharks shake off some of their lethargy to score through Van Rensburg, Brosnihan and the returning Garvey, who scores after only two minutes on the field.

Continuing their major failing in the Super 12 the Sharks fail to turn possession and territorial superiority into the valuable bonus point and at the end of the game are thrown into desperate defence as the Falcons belatedly begin to believe in themselves.

The most entertaining performance of the evening comes from replacement referee, Louis Mzomba, who deputises when Andy Turner pulls a hamstring. Waving his arms and gesticulating like a concert conductor he gives some bemusing decisions and manages to get in the way of play on countless occasions.]

Adrian Garvey celebrated his return from an achilles injury with a try only a couple of minutes after taking the field. Replacement referee Mzomba directs him towards the try line.

vs North West

vs North West

The Sharks 54 vs North West 15, *The Stadium, Kings Park, Durban, June 11*

Sharks: *Bennett, Payne, Halstead, Gillingham, Swart, VD Westhuyzen, Martens, Brosnihan, Fyvie, van Rensburg, Slade, Wegner, Moyle, Rossouw, Whittingham*

North West: *De Jager, Fredericks, Muller, Rohrs, VD Berg, Calitz, Verster, Pool, Rohrs, De Beer, Lessing, Stoltz, Redelinghuys, Van Rensburg, Human*

With all due respect to North West the Sharks treat this as a practice match. After the disappointingly flat performance the week before they are determined to put some points on the board and play with a lot more fluidity.

The first-half goes exactly according to plan. A couple of minutes to subdue the North West pack and then running the ball wide at every opportunity.

Seven tries in the first-half, a couple of them length of the field efforts, ensure that there will be no repeats of the previous week's fraught performance.

There is a gaping gap in class particularly in the back-line. Swart and Payne are at the centre of most of the Sharks attacks, and enjoy more possession than they have seen all season.

To their credit North West come back well in the second-half and out-score the home team.]

Left: *Captain Wayne Fyvie takes a break on the bench midway through the second-half.*

Above right: *Charl van Rensburg claims lineout possession.*

Right: *Shaun Payne on his way to a try.*

Below: *Mac hands Rex Elliott his first cap in the change room after the game.*

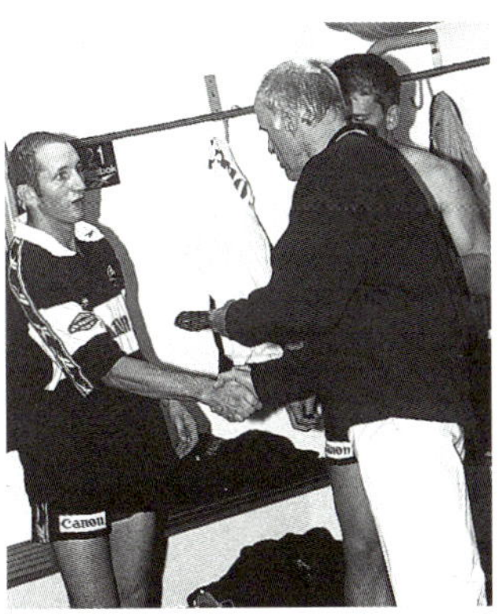

After Hours

Previous page: *Adrian Garvey takes a swim with the dolphins at Durban's Sea World as part of a fund-raising campaign.*

Clockwise from top left: *John Smit is forced to celebrate his 21st on the plane back from East London;* *The back-room staff at Auckland's Eden Park;* *Hugh Reece-Edwards and Mike Kelroe-Cooke enjoy a quiet pint after yet another win;* *Warren Brosnihan, André Joubert, Kevin Stevenson and Pieter Muller in the change room after the victory over the Blues;* *Ollie Le Roux lets off steam at Bourbon Street with long-suffering girlfriend Mariska at his side;* *Standing around on the runway in the freezing mist of East London;* *Mac leads the singing in the pub on the pre-season tour;* *Mornay Visser has a quiet nap in the hotel lobby while the rest of the team sit on the bus waiting for him;* *Stefan 'sweet smelling' Terblanche looking for gifts in a Brisbane duty-free shop;* *One-bounce, always one-bounce;* *Pieter Muller and Hentie Martens lead the singing after the Super 12 game against the Reds;* *Mornay Visser fulfils a long-held desire and pretends to be an air-hostess;* *Joe Gillingham, there is no more to say; Steve Felsher looks on as Warren Britz and Shaun Payne use his clean scissors to cut biltong;* *The 100 club, Mark Andrews and Adrian Garvey join John Slade as he celebrates 100 appearances after the semi-final;* *John Slade on a day-trip in New Zealand. It took him half-an-hour and 50 hits to the head before he realised what was going on.*

Reebok
SHARKS

SHISEIDO
Men's Fragrance

vs Griquas

vs Griquas

Sharks 23 vs Griqualand West 29, *ABSA Park Kimberly, 18 June*
Sharks: *Bennett, Payne, Gillingham, Halstead, Swart, VD Westhuyzen, Martens, Brosnihan, Britz, Slade, Wegner, van Rensburg, Moyle, Rossouw, Garvey*
Griquas: *vd Heever, Smith, Vermuelen, Strydom, Nicholas, Wessels, Husselman, Bakkes, Watts, Matfield, Smit, Brand, Theron, Cameron, Vermeulen*

Against Mac's better instincts the Sharks fly into Kimberly on the morning of the game. He would rather come in a day or two before and let the players settle. On the plane rugby isn't at the forefront of everyone's minds, they're more interested in South Africa's dramatic loss to Australia in the cricket World Cup.

Griquas won at Kings Park early last year and are now coached by ex-Natal Wildebeest coach Swys De Bruin. They obviously fancy their chances of upsetting the big boys again. Victories in Kimberly are hard enough to come by and the Sharks are missing most of their Springboks plus captain Wayne Fyvie is a late withdrawal with stomach flu. Hentie Martens takes over the captaincy.

In front of a sparse Friday afternoon crowd the fired-up Griquas side are given early encouragement when the Sharks knock-on directly from the kick-off. Within minutes Griquas fly-half Boeta Wessels goes over close to the posts.

Already the bench is looking edgy and the reporter from the Diamond Fields Advertiser is leaping out of his seat and shouting abuse at the ref. Bushie, the octogenarian Griquas mascot, is going crazy and you can hear Mac grinding his teeth.

They keep making basic errors and getting turned by kicks. The first 20 minutes are played out almost entirely in our half and Griquas extend their lead to 14 points. Finally just before half-time Brent Moyle crashes over.

Half-time brings no respite and within 15 minutes Griquas are 26-8 in front as their back row takes control. André Joubert comes on at fly-half in an attempt to regain some stability but they are missing the tackling and spoiling of captain Wayne Fyvie who has been outstanding this season.

Slowly things start to happen and with 10 minutes to go John Smit goes over after popping up at fly-half.

Just before the end Joe Gillingham breaks and goes over from 50 metres. It's a crucial score as it secures a bonus point, ensuring at least something from this desperately depressing trip.]

Right: *Full-back Russell Bennett launches a counter-attack. Schoolboys note — always carry the ball in two hands.*

Below: *Jaco van der Westhuyzen attempts to get past his opposite number, Boeta Wessels, during the first-half.*

GILBERT

Left: *Photographer Howard Cleland re-discovers his faith back on the ground at Kimberly airport. Pilot Don Muir begins to realise what might have been and calms himself down with a beer.*
Below: *Team management and committee members celebrate at the Spur.*

After the game we are cocooned in the dimly lit function room at Absa Park. Mould has destroyed many of the old photographs and the beer runs out disturbingly early.

Everyone is desperate to get home and Mike Kelroe-Cooke fumes on the phone as we are delayed further while they try to sort out a battery problem on the plane.

Spirits start to lift a little as the team look forward to getting home. Friday night in Durban beckons. Before we get on the plane, the new player initiation is held on the tarmac. I am sworn not to reveal exact details but suffice to say it involves a big stick and bending over. Trevor Halstead, Justin Swart and Brent Moyle are now officially Sharks.

A couple of minutes into the flight the right engine bursts into flame. There is a loud bang and a huge flash of light. First there is silence, then the sound of Joe Gillingham nervously laughing and finally Adrian Garvey shouting repeatedly for someone to tell the pilot.

The pilot knows exactly what is happening. His alertness means that the engine and fuel supply are shut down immediately. Slowly he turns us back towards Kimberly. He keeps the nose up so there is the strange feeling that maybe he is going to try and fly us to Durban on one engine, but then the runway comes back into view.

As we land Joe leads a chorus of "He's got the whole world in his hands," followed by a huge round of applause and hysterically relieved laughter.

Back in the terminal what happened, and what could have happened begins to sink in. A sense of humour always helps, "shit that was bad, but I bet I still don't feel as bad as Alan Donald," says Adrian Garvey.

One person who seems completely unaffected by it all is Shaun Payne who was sitting up front with the pilot and seems more excited than scared. Our pilot has a slight shake in his hands as he explains that had the engine blown a minute earlier we probably wouldn't have stayed in the air as there was insufficient thrust.

Justin Swart who hates flying is very quiet and our Aerospace rep is a complete wreck. Worse is to come when they tell us that we are going to have to fly again later that evening in an identical plane.

Our bus has disappeared so we climb on a re-treaded Putco bus and go back to the Spur in Kimberly. The delayed shock, euphoria of being alive and plenty of beer leads to many a raucous chorus of the Yogi Bear song.

Religious men are drinking tequila and party animals are discussing the nature of life, God, and the universe.

The flight back is somewhat of a haze. It's the only way we could get through it again. The next day surrounded by family, it begins to sink in, a sort of delayed shock as I realise how close to death we were.]

Boks vs Azzurri

The day after the Griquas game the Italian Azzuri arrive at Kings Park for their second test against the Springboks.

The Springboks, captained by Corné Krige in place of the injured Gary Teichmann, simply blow the Italians away.

A record test score of 101-0 takes the victory from the realms of a beating to the depths of a ritual slaughter. The Italians are missing virtually their entire backline and the Boks simply have too much class for them.

The only highlights of this woefully lopsided game are a record-breaking five-try performance from Stefan Terblanche and a hat-trick from debutant Deon Kayser.

As preparation for the challenge of Australia and New Zealand in the Tri-Nations series it doesno good. The Boks go on to suffer record defeats against both New Zealand and Australia as well as losing for the first-time ever to Wales.

Left from top:

Lock Selborne Boome goes high to claim a line-out;

Captain on the night Corné Krige leads the charge with support from Selborne Boome;

Sharks fitness adviser Kevin Stevenson fills the same position for the national squad;

Dave von Hoesslin, who joined the Sharks later in the season makes his debut against the Italians.

Right: *Record breaking try scorer Stefan Terblanche is the model of focus and concentration during the national anthems.*

SA RUGBY
SA vs ITALY
19/06/99

Canon

vs Blue Bulls

vs Blue Bulls

The Sharks 27 vs Blue Bulls 16, *Minolta Loftus, Pretoria, 27 June*
Sharks: *Bennett, Brink, Halstead, Gillingham, Swart, Joubert, Martens, Brosnihan, Fyvie, Andrews, Slade, van Rensburg, Garvey, Rossouw, Moyle*
Blue Bulls: *Goosen, Meyer, Olivier, Esterhuizen, Steyn, Smith, Breytenbach, Williams, vd Walt, Basson, Grobelaar, Kruger, Camphor, Brooks, Ribbens*

The team have been on the highveld for four days. After the Kimberly debacle/experience Mac has demanded that the team always fly in early, on a big plane, to away games. To further calm their nerves the team have spent a couple of days at Sun City golfing and relaxing.

The Bulls have been one of the Sharks hoodoo teams in the last few seasons, particularly at home. The last time the Sharks won in Pretoria was the 1990 Currie Cup final, Natal's first ever title and the foundation on which the McIntosh legend is built.

Minolta Loftus has a slightly surreal feel to it. 'Boere' disco booms around the disappointingly half-full stadium, fat men with moustache's hit each other with large blue foam fingers and the Blue Bulls body care range is launched. You can be sure some lucky relative will be receiving 'essence of Casper Steyn' aftershave this Christmas.

The curtain-raiser is the first competitive Under 21 game of the season. The NRU have invested a lot of money in developing younger talent and are beginning to receive dividends. The 'Junior Sharks' turn in a superb performance which serves as a great appetiser for the main game.

The Sharks welcome back Mark Andrews and André Joubert takes over at fly-half, a position he hasn't played for years. It is also Adrian Garvey's 100th appearance for the Sharks.

Both sides spend the first 15 minutes probing and the Bulls get the first points through a penalty. The Sharks pack is playing well, with the returning Andrews adding a bit of fire and aggression. After 20 minutes Russell Bennett rounds off a back row move to go over in the corner. Barely five minutes later Brink scores but Joubert misses a relatively simple conversion. Despite these misses Joubert has slotted in perfectly at fly-half. He keeps kicking into the corners, playing for territory and turning the Bulls. It's almost like watching Naas in his heyday.

Hooker Chris Rossouw makes two big breaks but on the first occasion drops the ball with nobody near him, and on the second passes to an invisible colleague. At least the Sharks are playing with a great deal of fluency and purpose.

Just before half-time the Bulls hit back when Steyn goes over to level the scores. The Bulls dominate the first 10 minutes of the second-half and build a six point lead. The Sharks pack come back hard and set up the platform for Joubert to start dictating. A delicate chip causes confusion and Stephen Brink steals in to score.

Two minutes later Hentie Martens makes a blind-side break from inside his own half, exchanges passes with Justin Swart and goes over in the corner. The Sharks have now scored four tries to one but are still only four points in front.

Inspired by Andrews the pack show plenty of grit and determination as they keep the Bulls pinned back in their own half for the rest of the game. Not even the introduction of the returning Joost Van der Westhuyzen who has been out since injuring his knee against England in December, can lift them.

Desperate to breakout the Bulls are starting to throw some pretty wild passes. One of these is intercepted by Joubert who caps an outstanding performance by gliding in under the posts. And he finally gets a conversion over.]

NASHUA

NASHUA

Previous page: *Centre Trevor Halstead breaks the tackle of Jacques Olivier. It was another impressive performance from the young centre.*

Top left x 2: *André Joubert who had a masterful game in the unfamiliar position of fly-half caps his performance with a try under the posts.*

Bottom left: *Trevor Halstead tries to keep the ball alive as the Sharks attack the Bulls line.*

Right: *One of the faithful, bathed in Blue Bulls 'eau de toilette' cheers his team on.*

Below: *From left. Charl van Rensburg, Warren Brosnihan, Mark Andrews and Justin Swart in the dressing room after the game.*

Canon
Canon
Reebok

André Joubert

André Joubert, a legend in his own 22. The end of the 1999 South African season sees the retirement of the incomparable full-back. He has a couple of nicknames within the team; Juba, Rolls and just occasionally, old man. He answers them all with a quiet, slightly mischievous, smile as he maintains the unruffled demeanour that sets him apart on the field.

TV commentators all seemingly reading the same script refer to him as 'the Rolls Royce of fullbacks.' Whatever you choose to call him there is no doubt he is one of the best full-backs ever to wear a Springbok jersey and probably, with all due respect to Hugh Reece-Edwards, the best ever in Sharks colours.

He is retiring completely from the game although he has said, if business interests allow, he would like to coach junior players. Like the men who are leaving at the same time as him, Teichmann and Honiball he was something of a late developer at both provincial and international level.

After moving from Free State to Natal he only cemented his position in the national side in 1994, which, with his usual impeccable timing, meant he was in pole-position when the 1995 World Cup kicked-off.

His performances in the tournament guaranteed that his name would go down in Bok history as one of the greats. In the quarter-final against Manu Samoa his hand was broken by a vicious late tackle. Undaunted he had surgery, and wearing a light-weight protective cast took his place in the 'underwater semi-final' the following week. In atrocious conditions, brought on by continual torrential downpours, the Springboks squeezed past the French with Joubert unflinching at the back. In the final he played his part to perfection as the Boks overcame the All Blacks after extra-time.

His scintillating form carried through into 1996 when he was instrumental in the Sharks winning their fourth Currie Cup title of the decade. In the final he scored two exquisite tries which perfectly emphasised the difference in class on the day between the Sharks and their opponents, Transvaal.

One of the highlights of this year for me was standing in the rain in Hamilton eating a dodgy hot dog that he bought for me. For Sean I think it was beating him at pool in Brisbane, no mean feat against someone with André's eye/hand co-ordination. Small moments but ones that mean so much.

André will be remembered by fans for his calm demeanour, the perfect positional sense, the safe hands, the long kicks with the left boot and his smooth speed as he joined the line.

But he will also be remembered as a perfect gentleman and grateful for what he has achieved. Humble as ever he expressed himself simply at the Ian McIntosh benefit dinner; "Thank you Mac, you made me the player I am."]

Left: *Juba in action during his final game, the Currie Cup final.*
Right: *The old and the new, John Smit gets his picture taken with Juba one last time after the final.*

vs Cheetahs

The Sharks 30 vs Free State Cheetahs 22, *The Stadium Kings Park, Durban, 9 July*
Sharks: *Joubert, Brink, Halstead, Gillingham, Swart, Honiball, Martens, Brosnihan, Fyvie, Atherton, Slade, van Rensburg, Garvey, Rossouw, Moyle*
Free State Cheetahs: *Korff, Badenhorst, Kruger, Venter, van Wyk, De Beer, Powell, Coetzee, Kasselman, Els, Beukes, Stander, Stander.M, Louw, Groenewald*

Friday night and perfect Durban winter weather, clear and mild, for this top-of-the-table clash. The Sharks have had a nice break, though tonight is the first of three games in a week.

The Cheetahs top the table despite losing a lot of key players in the close season, as they seem to every year. They have however been bolstered by the return of centre Brendan Venter and fly-half Jannie De Beer from the English Premiership. They continue to unearth exciting young players and play open, running rugby. If they could hang on to their players they would have certainly won a lot more Currie Cups.

The Sharks certainly look the fresher for their break and start well. From the kick off they run the ball back to the Cheetahs 22 and immediately start applying pressure.

After only three minutes the rapidly improving Trevor Halstead hands off De Beer and goes for the line. He brushes off four tacklers before reaching out and placing the ball over the line. Honiball converts and the Sharks are 7-0 up. Nothing seems to faze the Free Staters though and they come straight back. It all makes for great watching if a little nerve-wracking at times.

Ex-Free Stater Charl van Rensburg is having a huge game against his former province and putting in plenty of work. A Garvey try is disallowed by the erratic André Watson before De Beer and Honiball trade penalties. Badenhorst then goes over and the Cheetahs are right back in it. For a ten minute period the Sharks can't get their hands on the ball. Referee Watson continues to make some bizarre decisions and even gets a shake of the head from the eternally phlegmatic Henry Honiball.

Just before half-time Joe Gillingham scores an almost identical try to the one he scored against Otago in the Super 12. Honiball makes the break after quick ball from a line-out and puts Joe in under the posts. The half-time break sees the Sharks go in 20-16 in front.

A couple of minutes after the re-start there is yet another great piece of skill from Charl van Rensburg to send the increasingly predatory Justin Swart over in the corner. The pack are starting to out-muscle the Cheetahs and the loose trio are playing magnificently.

Hooker Chris Rossouw is another having a great game. His work rate is high as he seems always available to carry the ball as the forwards punch big holes in the Cheetahs defence around the ruck and maul fringes.

The indiscipline which often seems to affect the Cheetahs begins to creep into their game. The Sharks attempt a quick throw-in at a lineout. Warren Brosnihan makes the catch and is then nearly decapitated as the flying Jaco Coetzee smashes an elbow into his head. Luckily 'Bros' is wearing a scrum-cap so there is no major damage.

Incredibly the incident is either missed or completely ignored by Watson and his touch judges. There is no yellow card and a penalty is given for coming in from the wrong side, not for dangerous play. It begs the question of what exactly he was doing or watching at the time? As Brosnihan was in possession of

Right: *Adrian Garvey and Nico Wegner take a quick breather while waiting at a lineout.*

RUGBY
Canon
Canon

Left: *Trevor Halstead breaks through tackles and maintains his balance on his way to scoring the games opening try.*
Right: *Wayne Fyvie mauls the ball forward with the help of Steve Atherton (left) and Charl van Rensburg.*
Below: *Joe Gillingham bursts through the Cheetahs defence to score under the posts.*

the ball one would imagine that the referee's eyes, and those of the other officials, would be on him.
The Sharks keep their cool even though the ever accurate De Beer keeps the Cheetahs in touch with another penalty. Directly from kick-off there is some inspired play from Joe Gillingham which sets up an attacking scrum on the Cheetahs line. A slick back-row move leads to a try from Fyvie.
The intensity of the game begins to take its toll and both Joubert and Gillingham leave the field, while Henry Honiball makes yet another trip to the blood-bin. Trevor Halstead looks exhausted and very keen to come off but there are no more backs left on the bench so he has to stay on.
The Cheetahs are now running the ball from anywhere which causes a few anxious moments. It takes a trademark huge Honiball tackle on Chris Badenhorst to settle everything down.
Five points in the bag and a job very well done sends the Sharks onto the road in great heart.]

NBS

Canon
vodacom

vs Griffons

Sharks 45 vs Griffons 19, *NFS Stadium, Welkom, 13 July*
Sharks: *Bennett, Swart, Halstead, Payne, Brink, van Rensburg Cl, Martens, Brosnihan, Fyvie, van Rensburg, Atherton, Slade, Garvey, Visser, Moyle.*
NFS Griffons: *Coetzer, Pieters, De Jager, Abbott, Passens, Eigner, De Kock, Rabie, Pfister, du Toit, Raubenheimer, De Kock J, Diedericks, van Biljon, Appelgyn*

Twelve Hundred kilometres in a little red car with no signposts, no music and a sore back but at least we get to see the Sharks get the five points. The days of Welkom being a bogey venue for Natal teams is history and no longer are NFS a team of grim, gnarled miners, farmers and ex-security policeman.

This season they have gone for youth and brought in U21 players who may have been overlooked by the bigger provinces. They are young and like to run the ball from just about anywhere. With more weight in the pack they would definitely cause problems for a lot more teams. As it stands they are second from bottom of the log.

The Sharks backline changes as Honiball has a sore hamstring, Gillingham a slight groin strain and Joubert has injured his left knee. The pack is unchanged except for Mornay Visser getting a run.

Mac hates these games. The Sharks are expected to win but it is difficult to motivate the players. Once you are used to playing in front of 30 000 plus every week it is difficult to have the same intensity in front of 1500.

In the first half the Sharks are comfortably in control but are sloppy in their execution. Three tries give them the lead but the Griffins kick a couple of penalties to stay in touch. The second half starts with the Sharks running in a try from a scrum on their own line. Martens breaks blind and then on to Brink who strolls in for the bonus point. Instead of precipitating a rout, it only inspires NFS who take control for the next half-hour. Wing Giscard Pieters rounds off a field length move and suddenly the Griffons are within a converted try of the Sharks.

For half-an-hour the Sharks are ordinary and it is only in the final ten minutes that they run in a further three tries. The introduction of Chris Rossouw seems to galvanise the pack to secure, what is in the end, a comfortable win.

The team aren't happy with their performance but glad of the five points. It's on to Wellington for their third game in a week.]

Above: *A messy scrabble on the floor for possession is indicative of the game.*
Right: *While the Griffons don't have many supporters they certainly have some of the biggest.*
Far right: *The view from the main stand.*
Next page: *The team say a short prayer after the game.*

Reebok

Canon

Reebok

vs Cavaliers

The Sharks 34 vs Boland Cavaliers 28, *Boland Stadium, Wellington, July 16*
Sharks: *Bennett, Payne, Halstead, Gillingham, Swart, Honiball, Davidson, Brosnihan, Fyvie, Slade, Wegner, van Rensburg, Garvey, Rossouw, Moyle*
Boland Cavaliers: *Malherbe, Daniels, Joubert, van Jaarsveld, Ackerman, Whiston, Roux, Nelson, Kock, Maree, Julies, Coetzee, vd Merwe, Santon, Marais*

The end of the trilogy. Three games in a week, and two too many according to captain Wayne Fyvie. A win will put the Sharks at the top of the log for the first time this season.
On a dreary day of intermittent sun and blustery rain showers the tiny Boland Stadium is friendly but unfortunately reeks of freshly laid manure. The Natal U21's play their Boland counterparts in the curtain-raiser winning impressively again, 42-11. They run the ball well on a difficult, sodden pitch.
The midfield is beefed up by the return of Henry Honiball and Joe Gillingham. The Sharks start badly when a Honiball clearance is charged down, the hugely impressive John Daniels collects and scores under the posts.
It does however wake them up and they begin to attack fluently and score three tries in 10 minutes through Russell Bennett and two from Warren Brosnihan.
The back row and new scrum-half Craig Davidson are combining well. Concentration lapses though and an untidy lineout lets the Cavaliers score again. Mac is getting a little irate and his shouts of despair and frustration can be heard echoing around the empty ground.
The Sharks start the second half with a try from Shaun Payne after a great break from Honiball. The lead only serves to inspire the Cavaliers who score directly from the kick-off. Despite two Honiball penalties in the last 10 minutes the Sharks have to dig deep, particularly in the forwards as the Cavaliers attack incessantly. Daniels scores again in injury time, using sheer speed to round Bennett, but the Sharks take home the points.
After the game the players join members of the Cape-based Sharks supporters club in a room under the stand to celebrate victory before heading back to the bright lights of Cape Town and then home.]

Left: *Craig Davidson counter-attacks in his first full game for the Sharks.*
Below: *It was standing room only at the Boland Stadium.*

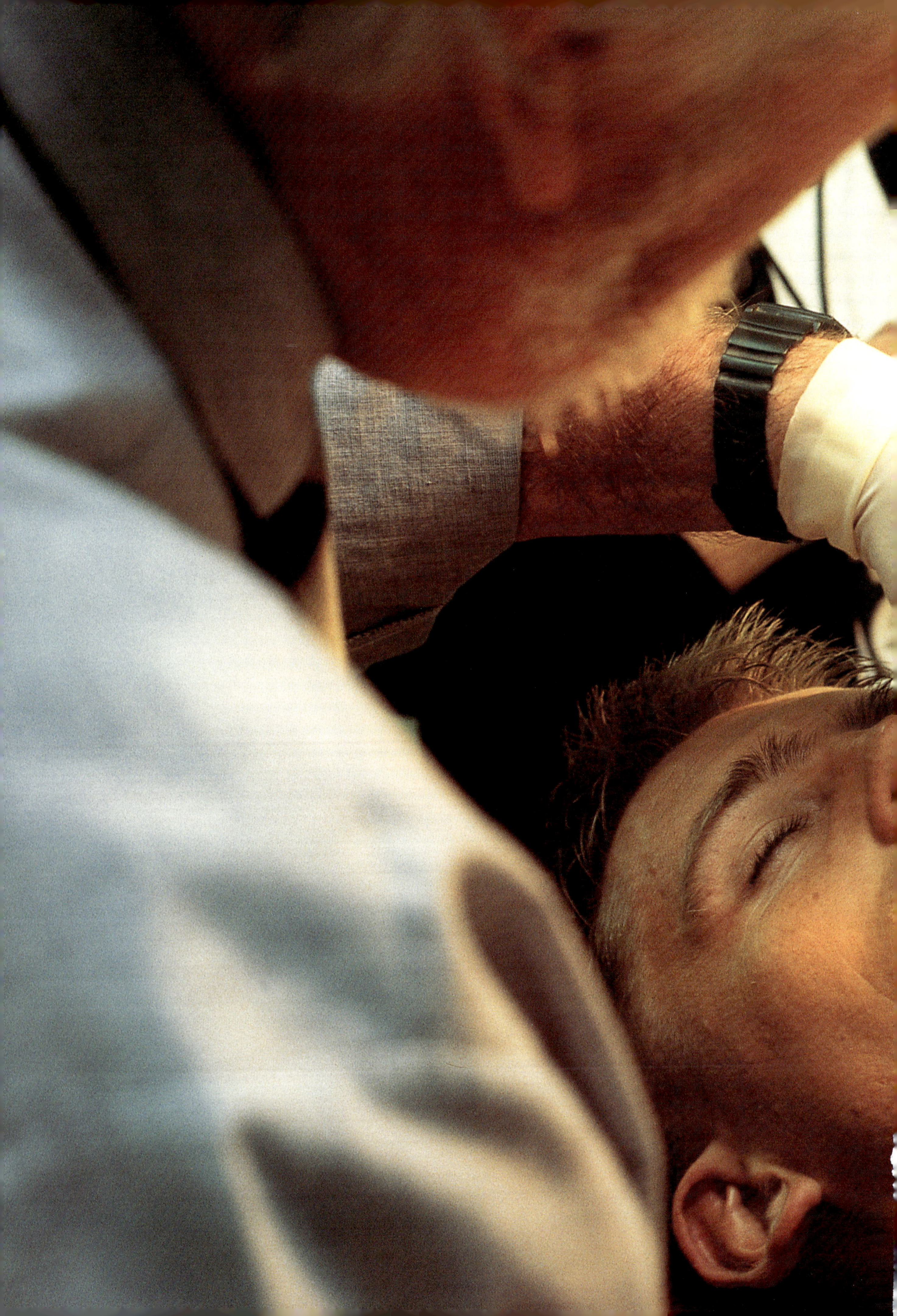

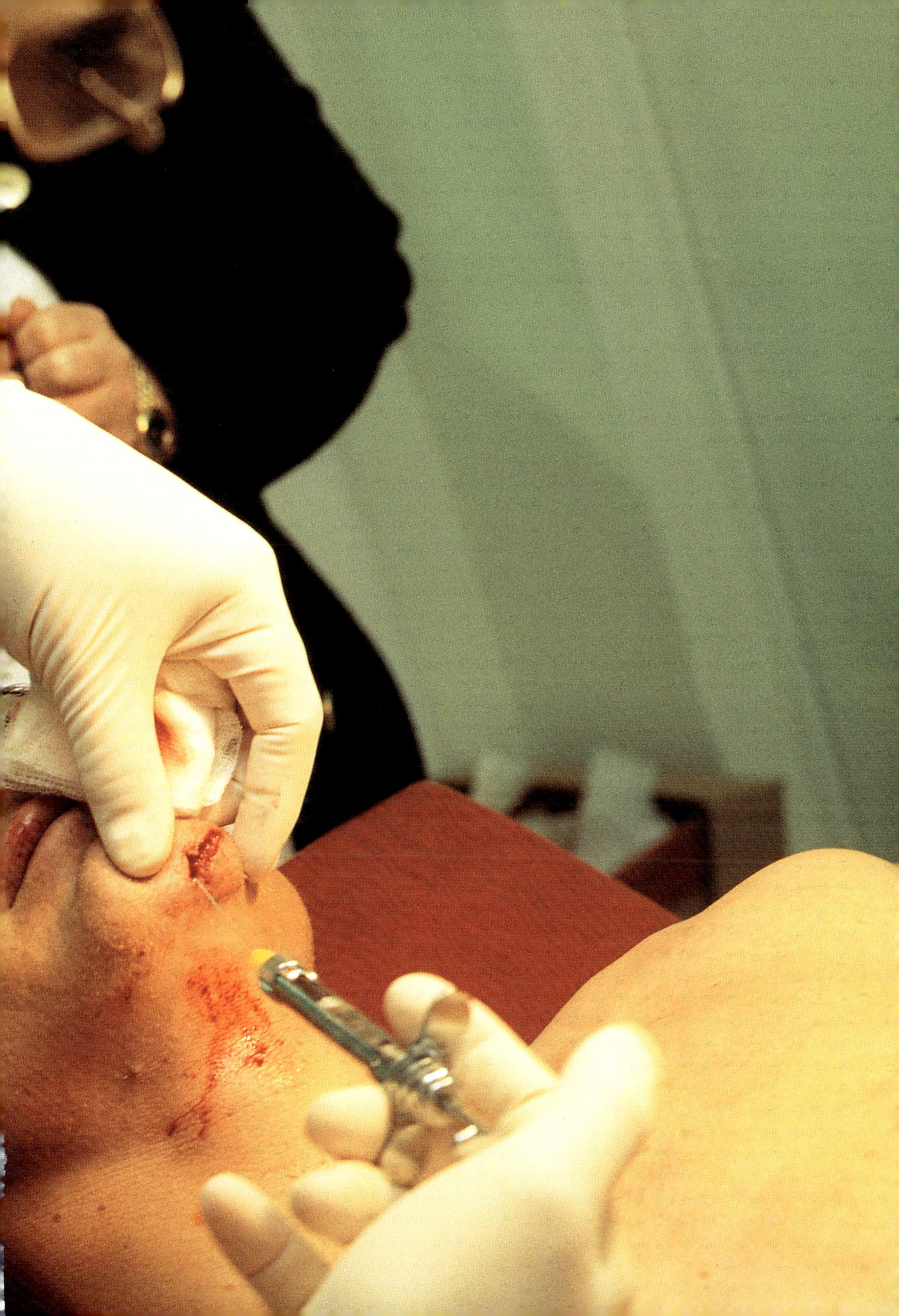

Blood Bin

The medical team are the unsung heroes of the Sharks set-up. Team doctor Dr Glen Hagemann, physiotherapists Steve Felsher and Dave Becker and fitness trainers Kevin Stevenson and Barry Angus provide a professional back-up as they are all acknowledged experts in their field. Contracted on a yearly basis they are at the top of their professions.

Seemingly on call 24 hours a day they only step into the limelight as they ferry water to the players and apply the 'magic sponge' during the game. On match days they start strapping and massaging the players at least two hours before the game starts.

Despite being frequently on the field during a game they often miss most of the action and the tries as they are either treating someone or making sure there are no injured bodies behind the play.

They are also relied upon to pass messages from the coaching staff to the players. As you can imagine they often bear the brunt when there is a mistake. As they are fond of saying; if the team win it's because of the coach, but if they lose it's the doctors and physio's fault for not preparing them properly.

They are all close in age to the players so there is a great rapport and they also provide a mental as well as physical back-up. Players can get down about injuries and minor niggles and worry that they won't be at their best. The medical staff have a role to play as ad hoc psychologists as they massage delicate egos and provide constant affirmation for those who are a little unsure.

The others will disagree but I think the physio's have the toughest job. While in Australasia the sheer physical slog of deep massaging the extremely muscled bodies of 15 to 25 men a day, meant that Steve saw New Zealand in a less than favourable light, if he saw it at all.

The Sharks Medical Centre housed at the Kings Park Health & Racquet club is newly opened and is further proof that the welfare of the players is becoming ever more important.

It is invariably busy with facilities to treat up to six players at once. An additional treat for the players is the once weekly visit of a team of sports masseurs.]

Previous Page: *Shaun Payne has an injection before receiving stitches in his chin after the game.*
Below from left:
Gary Teichmann goes off during the final for some running repairs to a cut in his head;
Steve Felsher relays a bit of advice to Clinton van Rensburg;
Barry Angus with the all important water for Ollie Le Roux.
Right: *John Slade gets the healing effects of the magic water.*

SHARKS
RUGBY
Reebok
Canon

THE STADIUM KINGS PARK
Clover
Canon
VAN NIEKERK
Wolf Security

Up & Coming

The Natal Rugby Union are renowned as great planners and innovators with perhaps their most significant initiative being the development of a structured youth development programme.

With the split in the Union, into commercial and rugby divisions, even more emphasis will be placed on developing young talent. The rugby division under Peter Smith will focus on club, development and youth rugby. It makes sense from both a rugby and financial perspective to develop home-grown talent.

A co-ordinated coaching structure from U14 right through to senior level has been established with elite squads at U14, U15 and U16 level. These squads undergo regular trials and fitness assessments to maintain progress. The Union, through director of coaching Garth Giles, works closely with schools and is indebted to the time and effort put in by the teachers who have helped ensure that the programme has been a success.

Players then move to the U18, newly developed U19, and U21 squads. This continuity ensures that young players adapt to a structured coaching style and playing framework at an early age. The U19's encouragingly made the final of their competition, but lost to the Blue Bulls.

A few seasons ago the Union also took the decision to recruit promising talent from around the country. Money is spent on developing young players rather than just constantly buying ready-made senior players.

This progressive policy has begun to reap rewards with eight players representing the U21 Springboks in the mini-World Cup in Argentina. The team was captained by John Smit who has already established himself in the senior squad. Other notable squad members include Shaun Sowerby, Frikkie Welsh, Piet Myburgh, Butch James and Jaco van der Westhuyzen.

Despite missing many of their leading lights the U21 side comfortably made the final of the U21 competition. Under the coaching of Charles Louw and management of Gavin Melvill they played open attractive rugby that was always great to watch.

Unfortunately in the against the Lions they put in probably their least impressive performance of the season and were well beaten on the day.]

Left: *Sharks U21 prop Aubrey Mbatha and Lions captain Pietman van Niekerk walk off the field after the final.*

Right: *The U21's get a pep-talk from Mac after victory over the Blue Bulls at Minolta Loftus.*

vs Border

The Sharks 50 *vs* ***Border Bulldogs 24****, The Stadium Kings Park, Durban, 25 July*
The Sharks*: Bennett, Terblanche, Halstead, Gillingham, Swart, Honiball, Davidson, Brosnihan, Fyvie, Slade, Wegner, van Rensburg, Garvey, Rossouw, Moyle*
Border: *Weyer, Maidza, Gelderbloom, Pickering, Malotana, vd Merwe, Bennett, vd Walt, Swart, Kockjeu, Botha, Jacobs, Swanepoel, Du Preez, Kok*

The run-up to the game has been put into perspective by the tragic death of Steve Atherton's brother Jason during the week. The crowd observe a moments silence before the game starts.
Springbok wing Stefan Terblanche makes a return to the side with both Payne and Brink unlucky to lose their places. Border are having a mini-resurgence stringing together a couple of victories including one over the Blue Bulls.
The Sharks start slowly and after 15 minutes thy are 10-0 down after a superb run by new Springbok Kaya Molatana. Going behind wakes the Sharks up and they get on the board after Trevor Halstead, once more showing great strength, scores under the posts.
As a further boost there is a bit of a fracas with captain Wayne Fyvie throwing the most telling punch. This puts a bit of fire into the pack and soon after an effective blind-side move, it worked against Boland and NFS, leads to Bennett scoring against his old team. Unfortunately there is another lapse in concentration as Border score after an effective forward drive.
The Sharks come back strongly and Justin Swart scores after showing great strength and brushing off a couple of tackles. Just before half-time Joubert replaces the injured Bennett to great applause.
The Sharks secure the bonus point through a Halstead try and then Swart gets a second. The Sharks are showing plenty of commitment and to his obvious delight Davidson gets his first home try. André Joubert is keeping the ball in front of the forwards and Henry Honiball is throwing himself about with relish.
Border refuse to give up and remain competitive but they are clearly out-classed. Justin Swart gets his hat-trick after great sleight of hand from Honiball and Halstead and with it brings up the 50 point mark.
As a perfect example of the squad ethic that makes the Sharks so formidable, replacement wing Stephen Brink shows marvellous commitment in injury time as he chases down the flying David Maidza and stops him a metre short of the line.

Right: *Craig Davidson celebrates his first senior try at Kings Park in exuberant fashion.*
Left: *Henry Honiball and Joe Gillingham in tandem as they try to break through the Border defence.*

vodacom
CURRIE
Bankfin
CUP
Canon

Gary Teichmann

Gary Teichmann has in the past few seasons achieved iconic status in Natal as well as international rugby.

A thorough gentleman he is only confrontational and abrasive on the rugby field. The enormous hurt and disappointment he felt at his abandonment by Springbok coach Nick Mallet was hidden during the latter half of the season behind a dignified facade and a single-minded commitment to the Sharks.

There had been rumours of his impending dismissal for a while as Mallet, mesmerised by the Stormers impressive, yet ultimately disappointing, Super 12 performances sought to clear the way for Bobby Skinstad, and more bizarrely Anton Leonard.

Many people had an inkling of what was going to happen but when the news was confirmed, there were gasps of incredulity across the province and more tellingly from most of the rugby playing world. In Natal the outcry was loudest as he is deeply respected and has been integral to three of the Sharks Currie Cup triumphs in the 90's.

> *"at the moment I consider him to be the sixth best no 8 in the country"*
>
> *Nick Mallett*

Tellingly, as an insight into the divisions that still divide the provinces and social groupings, the English language newspapers were up in arms while the Afrikaans papers were muted and indifferent in their disapproval.

Joost vd Westhuizen, looking slightly overwhelmed, was named captain only a week after Mallett said he had no intention of rushing him back into the international arena.

Gary himself inherited the Springbok captaincy after Francois Pienaar was marginalised by André Markgraaf. He retained the captaincy, and even grew in stature, despite home series losses to the All Blacks and the British Lions. He maintained his form under the muddled coaching of Carel du Plessis and was at the fulcrum of the renaissance in the Bok's playing fortunes.

In 1998 he led the Springboks to the Tri-Nations title for the first time and on a record equalling 17 match unbeaten run. He was voted International Player of the Year in both Australia and New Zealand, and enjoyed almost universal respect among the rugby fraternity. Things changed after defeat by England and Gary's injury interrupted his start to the season. Rushed back into the side he was put under pressure to prove himself and suffered another injury.

As one of the most decent men to play the game his treatment reflected badly on Mallet and destroyed the air of integrity he had originally brought to the position when he was appointed to replace du Plessis.

During the entire season I have never seen Gary turn down a request for an autograph, nor have I seen him lose his temper when he is inevitably accosted by the odd 'expert' after a game.

Perhaps the most telling comment of the week came from Mac: "I'm sure Nick has made his mind up, which is a coaches prerogative. But I'm telling you that come the semi-finals in September Gary will be back to his old self." And how prophetic his words will come to be seen. While he should be leading the World Cup challenge he will instead be helping Newport as they attempt to re-establish themselves as a force in Welsh rugby.

The final comment from Gary highlights his self-belief and integrity; "I'm sad I'm missing the World Cup but I'll just concentrate on helping the Sharks win the Currie Cup. Life goes on."]

vs Lions

The Sharks 25 vs Golden Lions 17*, The Stadium Kings Park, Durban, 31 July*
The Sharks: *van Rensburg Cl, Payne, Halstead, Gillingham, Brink, Joubert, Davidson, Teichmann, Fyvie, Andrews, Slade, van Rensburg, Garvey, Visser, Moyle*
Golden Lions: *Engelbrecht, Williams, vd Walt, Mulder, Delport, Smith, Johnstone, Venter, Minaar, Strydom, Thorne, vd Merwe, Moore, Dalton, Mostert*

The week before this game has been dominated by the reaction to the sacking, for that's what it was, of Gary Teichmann from the Springbok side. There is plenty of anti-Mallet feeling around the braais in the car parks before the game, with one group of loyal fans wearing T-shirts with a particularly blunt message (*see overleaf*).

The Lions are coached by former All Blacks coach Laurie Mains. They have been one of the form teams of the season and have already won the Vodacom Cup, the provincial competition held during the Super 12. The Lions also have a number of players who have been ignored by Nick Mallet, among them the World Cup winners Hennie Le Roux, Hannes Strydom, Chester Williams and the excellent, and as yet un-capped, AJ Venter.

The spotlight remains on Teichmann as he catches the kick off. Both sides are very tight defensively and it takes an intercept from Shaun Payne to get the Sharks out of their own half. The Lions pack are playing aggressively, with former Bok hooker James Dalton prominent, and after taking the ball through several phases AJ Venter goes over.

Clinton Van Rensburg, a late replacement at full-back for the Sharks takes over kicking duties and puts over a penalty. He is something of a throwback as he uses sand and not a kicking tee. The Lions reply immediately when Chester Williams makes a great break which results in a try for captain Hannes Strydom.

After half-an-hour the Sharks get the break they need when Craig Davidson intercepts at the base of the scrum and races away to score in the corner. Luck also favours them when the dangerous Thinus Delport is pulled down barely a metre from the line. The big crowd is utterly absorbed by the contest and the

Previous page: *AJ Venter gets Trevor Halstead in a head lock.*

From left: *The Nick Mallet Appreciation Society; The bouncers at the One Stop pub in the north-west corner of The Stadium keep an eye on the wheely bins; Put your hands in the air and wave them like you just don't care; Mike Greenaway (hands in air), the Warren Beatty of South African rugby writing, celebrates as the Under 21's register a dramatic victory.*

Below: *Charl van Rensburg, to the despair of Hannes Strydom, scores a decisive try just before half-time.*

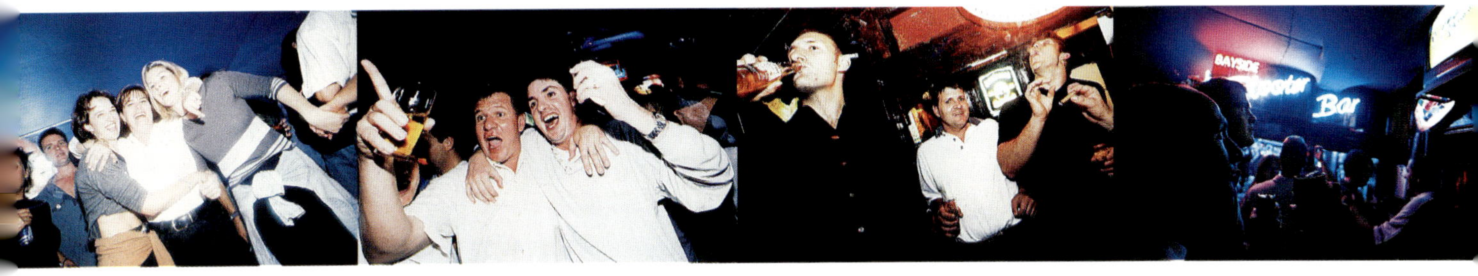

From left: *The better halves of Messrs Teichmann, Slade and Garvey let their hair down at 80's, the night-club/pub adjacent to the ground;* *Way hey, Nico Wegner (left) enjoys a beer while Kevin Schraader(right), savours a fine cigar;* *The game on the TV almost interrupts the general drinking and carousing.*

stadium is strangely quiet as they concentrate on the action.

Two minutes before half-time Teichmann wins a lineout and puts Charl van Rensburg into space. Van Rensburg bursts through the gap between two tacklers and reaches for the try-line to score.

At the start of the second-half Matt Pennefather briefly comes on to replace Joe Gillingham who is in the blood bin and the Sharks pick up where they left off in the first. André Joubert is kicking the ball huge distances and keeping the Lions pinned in their own half. A period of sustained pressure is only relieved when a penalty in front of the posts is reversed after Brent Moyle is caught throwing a punch.

The Lions immediately exploit this lucky break and great handling in the backs puts Williams over in the corner. The Sharks reply immediately when Shaun Payne intercepts a speculative MJ Smith pass and has a clear run in from 50 metres. Shortly after this van Rensburg puts over another penalty to extend the lead to eight points.

The Lions try hard to score but the Shark's defence is resolute. Mark Andrews is at the heart of the action, relishing the physical challenge and finishing a game for the first time this season. Young Craig Davidson deservedly wins the man-of-the-match award and is plainly already a big favourite with the crowd.

There is a great deal of celebration after the game as you get the feeling that people are finally starting to believe that the Sharks can achieve something this season. As a further fillip that evening everyone watches the Springbok Under 21's , led by Shark John Smit, beat their New Zealand counterparts with a last minute try. Another round of drinks my good man.]

vs Eagles

***The Sharks 18 vs SWD Eagles 22**, Outeniqua Park, George, 8 August*

***The Sharks:** van Rensburg CI, Swart, Payne, Halstead, Brink, Joubert, Davidson, Teichmann, Fyvie, Andrews, Slade, van Rensburg, Garvey, Visser, Moyle*

***SWD Eagles:** Du Toit, Treu, Lubbe, Joubert, Munn, van Rensburg, Turvey, Leonard, Wasserman, Frank, Bosman, Hattingh, Human, Webb, Wagner*

Pride before the fall as they say. The Sharks arrive in George top of the log to meet a SWD Eagles team who have been a revelation this season. They are in the running for a place in the semi-finals so they have plenty to play for.

Their small compact ground can be intimidating although having the home team run on to the field to the homo-erotic disco anthem, 'It's Raining Men' does dilute the effect a little.

After the excellence of last week's performance the Sharks are disappointingly flat and struggle to get going. The Eagles predictably enough are full of aggression and try to unsettle the Sharks, particularly in the pack with Human and Bosman constantly bordering on the illegal and downright dirty.

After trading penalties the Sharks get their first try when Mornay Visser goes over unimpeded in the corner after a slick lineout move. Both fly-halves are former Bok full-backs and they are both playing old-style rugby — kicking for position to keep the opposition in their own half.

The Eagles get within one point after another successful penalty but then immediately concede a try. Joubert takes the kick-off blind and catches them cold. Payne collects and passes inside to Joubert who goes over in the corner. The score seems to motivate the Eagles and they start to apply real pressure. They put pressure on the half-backs and it's clear that the Sharks are missing the physical presence of Gillingham and Muller in the centre. Under pressure Halstead has a kick charged down and Anton Leonard flops over.

Two minutes later Du Toit easily side steps Brink and runs 60 metres to score. A van Rensburg penalty keeps the Sharks in touch but they are now running the ball desperately to no avail.

At the end the celebrations are long and loud as the Eagles do a lap of honour.]

***Below:** Probably the best game of the afternoon. Mini-rugby before the game.*

***Right:** Gary Teichmann takes a tackle as he attempts to drive forward.*

***Overleaf:** John Slade puts in a big tackle.*

Bankfin
CUP
Bankfin
CUP

SHARKS
Canon

Canon
Canon

vs Elephants

The Sharks 16 vs EP Elephants 22, *Telkom Park, Port Elizabeth 15 August*

The Sharks: *Bennett, Payne, Halstead, Muller, Brink, Joubert, von Hoesslin, Teichmann, Fyvie, Slade, Atherton, van Rensburg, Garvey, Visser, Moyle*

EP Elephants: *Laubscher, Heidtman, Fourie, De Jager, Lombard, Bouwer, Alcock, Greeff, Pinnock, Swart, Rossouw, van Jaarsveld, Nel, Venter, vd Merwe*

The manner in which you win is often forgotten and becomes less important as you look at the points on the board. The manner in which you lose however is always important and is never forgotten.

The Sharks loss in Port Elizabeth was both embarrassing and inept. Leading from the start to one minute from the end they were lethargic and complacent. The Mighty Elephants, who scored three tries to one, deserved to win if only because they looked as if they wanted to.

As a welcome to next seasons newly appointed Sharks head coach Hugh Reece-Edwards, it probably made him feel like resigning.

A disappointing scenario is being replayed. The Sharks set the pace and then rob themselves of momentum by losing games they really should win at the end of the regular season. It happened in 1997 in the Currie Cup and again last year in both the Currie Cup and Super 12.

The selection of new arrival Dave Von Hoesslin at scrum-half over find-of-the-season Craig Davidson is a crucial selection error as the new boy struggles to clear his lines and communicate with his team-mates all game. One can't lay the blame entirely at his door as he is yet another player robbed of form by inactivity in the unlamented Springbok squad system. There is a lack of fire in the front five and Russell Bennett looks as if his return from a groin strain has come much too soon. Tackles are missed, but more crucially, so are vital touch kicks at the end of the game.

To lose to this desperately ordinary Elephants side was made more disappointing by the impact it may yet have on semi-final positions. The Cheetahs and Lions now have pole position and both look to be running into serious form.

The Sharks dominate comfortably enough at the start and score a simple try from Stephen Brink after working the blind side. Despite taking the lead they are never able to open up a gap and allow the EP pack to slowly gain control.

With a minute remaining EP have one last scrum on the Sharks 10 yard line. Everyone assume a drop kick is coming but instead Greeff charges from the back of the scrum and sets up a ruck in the 22. With the Sharks in disarray the ball is moved down the line for Laubscher to beat a despairing Garvey dive and score in the corner. To make matters worse the try is converted. For the second week in a row the Sharks walk off the field heads bowed as their triumphant opponents do a lap of honour.]

Left: *The returning Pieter Muller was his usual aggressive self but even he couldn't spark the Sharks.*

Below: *The Elephants bench celebrate their last-minute victory.*

vs Western Province

The Sharks 65 vs Western Province 29, *The Stadium Kings Park, Durban, 21 August*

The Sharks: *Joubert, Terblanche, Gillingham, Muller, Swart, Honiball, Martens, Teichmann, Fyvie, van Rensburg, Andrews, Slade, Garvey, Rossouw, Le Roux*

Western Province: *Paulse, Theron, Barry, Linee, Stevens, van Straaten, van Zyl, Roux, Brink, Barrett, van Heerden, Gerber, Hanekom, Marais, vd Linde*

There is animosity in the air and Kings Park is at its atmospheric best for the visit of Western Province. The Sharks have been given permission to play all their Springboks while Province have been told to rest theirs, thus letting Nick Mallett side-step any embarrassing comparisons in positions such as full-back, wing and no 8.

In the past couple of seasons a good deal of animosity has developed between the teams which has even seeped through to the upper echelons of the respective administrations. The presence of the SARFU media liaison officer on the Province bench provides discomforting evidence of the alleged favouritism and bias within South African rugby.

Mark Andrews leads the side out for his 100th appearance to thunderous applause from the 36 000 crowd. Despite all the encouragement the Sharks start very slowly and for the first 15 minutes can't get out of their own half. Western Province who have had a poor season start cohesively and score a good try in the corner after eight minutes.

Eventually the Sharks reply through Justin Swart who runs over Breyton Paulse on his way to the line. Province reply five minutes later as Toks vd Linde barges over and the crowd are beginning to get restless, the previous two weeks performances preying on their minds.

A Honiball penalty to level the scores provides the catalyst. Province kick blind and superb interplay between Swart, Honiball and Terblanche leads to a ruck on the Province line and eventually Andrews strolls, and I mean strolls, over in the corner.

A few minutes later Garvey squeezes over after a tapped penalty. From the resulting kick-off Britz, Muller, and Teichmann combine to send Charl van Rensburg over under the posts. It is a superb move and in an extremely rare show of emotion Teichmann punches the air in delight.

Province refuse to lie down and an intercept on his own line from Theron leads to a try. Five minutes later Paulse shows astonishing pace to round Joubert and go over under the posts for a try that puts the visitors back in striking distance.

[*"what did you think of Gary's performance ?" "solid."*

assistant Bok coach alan solomons]

The Sharks go up a gear again and Martens charges down a van Straaten clearance to score and then Swart, after a thrilling side-step from Joubert, goes over for his second try. Martens scores again as the Sharks, with the back-row at the centre of everything, begin to play with style and immense confidence .

Henry Honiball crosses to break the 60 point barrier before Robbie Brink gets a consolation try at the very end. It is a record victory for the Sharks and it certainly banishes the bad memories of the previous two weekends. The mood in the change-room afterwards is one of quiet satisfaction, of a job well done.]

Above: *Ollie Le Roux on the charge in his return to Sharks colours after a frustrating and relatively inactive sojourn with the Springboks.*
Below: *Joe Gillingham in the form of his life absorbs a tackle from Tinus Linee.*

Henry Honiball

Henry Honiball is a true enigma, a bona fide one-off. One of the hardest and most feared tacklers in the game, he is quiet, unassuming, excessively modest and almost gentle off the field. His humility is astonishing in one who has had so much praise and attention heaped on him, as is his ability to avoid the media and public spotlight.

The first time we met him was in a lift in Port Elizabeth before the Brumbies game. He towered over us, but just as big was his smile and warm greeting. He inspires affection and respect even in people who don't follow the game closely, much to his obvious embarrassment.

One of the more treasured memories of this season with the team was having a quiet drink with two greats Henry and André Joubert in a pub in Hamilton, New Zealand. Nobody said much, but it felt great.

Most people know him as 'Lem', Afrikaans for blade, for the way in which he scythes down the opposition. For a fly-half he is huge with an incredibly physical presence. The All Black Josh Kronfeld likens him and his impact on the game to having an 'extra flanker' on the field.

As a player he hasn't always been appreciated and it has only been in the past 18 months that he has firmly established himself as the Springbok fly-half. His prodigious defensive abilities have often been utilised at inside centre and the absolute commitment of his game has led to more than his fair share of injuries.

It is not widely known but he was almost lost to the game on two occasions. Firstly while attending Free State University he preferred to 'manage' his residence side rather than take part himself. Friends coerced him into playing in a trial game and soon he was collecting 37 caps for Free State.

In 1991 he returned to the family farm at Bergville in the foothills of the Drakensberg, his brief career apparently over. It took all the persuasive powers Mac could muster to get him playing again.

For Henry there is more than just the game and practice to consider. For the past eight years he has done a 400 km, four hour round trip, four times a week to fulfil his commitments and no one has yet heard him complain.

He also has the priceless ability to poke fun at himself. At Welkom as he sat watching the game a particularly persistent fan asked him how was his knee injury? "My knee is fine," replied Henry, "I just have to sort out my neck, shoulder, hip, hamstring and ankle, and I'll be fine."

After the 1999 World Cup he will play for Bristol in the English Premiership, a challenge he is looking forward to, although he is a little bemused that he is being paid a million rand to do so.

He is still genuinely surprised that he has managed to achieve so much in the game, and inspire such affection. He will be greatly missed in Natal, both in the dressing room and on the field.]

Canon
HONIBALL
10

BORG
Canon
Canon

Mr Price
VISSER

ROSSOUW
2

vs Pumas

***Sharks 50 vs Mpumalanga Pumas 15**, The Stadium Kings Park, Durban, 28 August*
***Sharks:** Bennett, Terblanche, Gillingham, Muller, Swart, van Rensburg CL, Martens, Teichmann, Fyvie, van Rensburg, Slade, Andrews, Garvey, Rossouw, Le Roux*
***Pumas:** Benadie, Fourie, Stoltz, Potgieter, Dames, Benadé, Bartle, Pretorious, Joubert, Stoltz.T, Willemse, Rossouw, Swart, Kemp, Joubert*

***Above:** Hentie Martens and Charl van Rensburg wait to pounce at a ruck.*
***Far Left:** Nico Wegner, who had a storming 20 minutes as a replacement goes high at a lineout.*
***Left:**Chris Rossouw gets hit by a double tackle.*
***Overleaf:** Stefan Terblanche on his way to scoring his second try of the night.*

The mood beforehand verges on the euphoric, though relief is probably the main emotion. The evening before the Falcons beat the Cheetahs handing the Sharks a home semi-final. It's the last Sharks game for the World Cup Springboks but Henry Honiball withdraws because of an ankle injury. Diffident as ever he shyly makes an appearance on the field to say farewell.

The Sharks carry on much as they left off last week. Initially they start slowly weathering early pressure from the big physical Pumas forwards before comfortably moving up several gears. van Rensburg is a revelation at fly-half, strong on his feet and always looking to attack.

For the second week running Gary Teichmann is in exceptional form, leading from the front as the team combine to play the 15-man rugby which is Mac's direct style at its best. At his shoulder is Charl van Rensburg, the most under-rated player in the country, who has been in superb form all season.

Stefan Terblanche is full of energy, getting involved all over the field, and tackling with relish, an area of his game that has improved markedly this season. In the centres Gillingham and Muller are playing with relish, doing the hard work, creating opportunities for those around them.

Five minutes after half-time the Sharks lead by 30 points and the most heartening sight of the evening is Ollie Le Roux shouting at his team-mates, urging them to further effort. Replacements come on and add extra drive with 'Big Nic' Wegner going over for only his second Sharks try.

The most poignant moment comes after the game in the change room when the departing Boks have their picture taken with Mac. The urge to usher Gary Teichmann into the picture is overwhelming, but he's staying here.]

All the sporting clichés apply. A sum of its parts, as strong as its weakest link. The Sharks are successful because first and foremost they are a team. Some players naturally receive more attention than others but for the Sharks each player is important. They have all had a part to play this season.

Clockwise from top left: *Mornay Visser the competitive and intense hooker who became a father for the first time early in the year; John 'Barney' Smit is one of the countries finest young talents as well as being one of the nicest; Stefan Terblanche has added crunching defence to his array of skills; Shaun Payne filled in at centre and wing grabbing a number of tries; Nico Wegner turned in some storming performances coming off the bench in the latter half of the season; Stephen Brink scored when given the opportunity but was unlucky with injuries; Russell Bennett wasn't always first choice but when he did play he invariably picked up the man-of-the-match award; Charl van Rensburg only missed one game all season and was a model of reliability and excellence; Matt Pennefather had a couple of runs coming off the bench — his un-sponsored Beetle is the coolest car in the side; Gavin Whittingham, with not a word of complaint, spent a season mainly on the bench; Pieter Muller was back to his fiery best this season but off the field he likes nothing better than a cuddle from Taryn, no really; Wayne Fyvie had an excellent season leading from the front; Craig McIntosh endured six consecutive games on the bench without getting on the field (ask dad); Ollie Le Roux had an impressive Super 12, but only appeared twice in the Currie Cup.*

Below left: *Justin Swart in his first season for the Sharks was the top try scorer with 12 and started to show some of the form that gained him his Springbok place.*

Below right: *Prop Brent Moyle moved from the Falcons at the start of the Currie Cup season and became an important member of the side.*

Right: *Quintessential Mark Andrews. Fiercely competitive, he started to play with some of his old form and fire this season and achieved 100 caps for the Sharks.*

JAWLERS
BEER GARDEN AND COFFEE SHOP

GSC

Fans

The Sharks are the best supported provincial or club team in the world. While other sides may occasionally draw bigger crowds no one can match the Sharks week in, week out support. With over 10 000 season ticket holders alone the Sharks inspire a loyal following and at no stage does crowd attendance drop below 15 000.

The CEO of Supersport Russell McMillan, who bought 40% of the Sharks for a staggering R43 million mid-way through the year, describes them as the Manchester United of rugby. A great analogy though the Sharks probably inspire more affection and less envy.

Match day at The Stadium is a unique experience in itself. Ballymore and Twickenham both have a tradition of pre-match barbecues and picnics, but neither can match the sheer scale of consumption and revelry seen before and after the game, on the eight fields outside the Stadium Kings Park.

Not many major stadiums have a night-club/pub in the ground as well as one 100 metres away. It says a lot for the supporters that there is very rarely any trouble.

The Sharks have also broken new ground in South African and world rugby in the past couple of years by being the first team to really exploit their success and develop a highly successful brand.

The Sharks logo can be found on everything from T-shirts to charcoal briquettes and, as can be seen on the right, on the arms of some of the more die-hard supporters.

After each game a number of players make appearances at the SharkTank, a stage, where they get to meet the fans.

The players are well aware of the role they play and the example they have to set. I have never seen one turn down a request for an autograph or be rude or abrupt.

Despite what at times can be the burden of constant exemplary behaviour they still manage to be approachable and enjoy themselves.

vodacom
6
Canon

Semi-Final

vs Cheethas

***The Sharks 45 vs Free State Cheetahs 8**, The Stadium Kings Park, Durban, 4 September*

***Natal Sharks:** Joubert, Payne, Halstead, Gillingham, Swart, van Rensburg CI, Martens, Teichmann, Fyvie, Slade, Atherton, van Rensburg, Moyle, Visser, Smit*

***Free State Cheetahs:** Korff, Badenhorst, Kruger, Du Toit, Horak, Fourie, Powell, Coetzee, Stander, Els, Beukes, de Klerk, Heymans, Louw, Groenewald*

The Sharks are fairly relaxed in the week before the final and make no significant changes to their routine. Swimming on Monday, training on KP2 on Tuesday, a captains practice on Thursday. On Friday evening they meet up at a hotel before going out to the cinema.

Dr Haggeman's reputation is in shreds, at least among other doctors, after a local paper reports that he gave Henry Honiball a Voltaren injection directly into his sore ankle, and not the usual place, his backside. If he had done, Henry would never play again, but at least he can have a laugh about it with the journalist, especially as another report comes out saying the players take three kg's of Creatine a day, not three grams.

The edgiest player in the side is John Slade who will be playing his 100th game for the Sharks. All week he pops copious quantities of vitamin pills to ward off sickness, and calm his nerves. He is determined not to let anyone down, especially as this has arguably been his best ever season and one in which he has appeared in every Currie Cup game.

There is a crowd of 44 000 as Slugger leads the team out to a huge roar. The Sharks start well but spurn the chance to go in front when van Rensburg hits the posts with a penalty from bang in front. A few minutes later he redeems himself by getting a kick over from a far more difficult position.

There is a moment of concern when Fyvie tackles Coetzee at an awkward angle and stays down holding his shoulder. Eventually he gets up and soldiers on.

There are a couple of problems in the front row with the Sharks coming under quite a bit of pressure. However the backline, in particular Halstead and Gillingham, are putting in some big hits, closing down space and not letting the Cheetahs back-line move the ball with any confidence.

Mornay Visser then makes one of his, fast becoming legendary, breaks to put the Sharks firmly on the attack. After an attacking lineout a superbly delayed pass from Clinton van Rensburg puts Halstead over under the posts.

There is a palpable sense of relief in both the crowd and the team. The Cheetahs look shaken and there is the feeling that they haven't fully recovered their confidence after losing the week before.

The Sharks immediately apply more pressure and set-up a lineout on the Cheetahs line. Teichmann peels around the front of the lineout and goes over with barely a hand laid on him. He is delighted as can be seen by his clenched fist salute.

After half-time the Sharks come out firing on all cylinders and the Cheetahs can barely hang on. A field-length move started by

Gary Teichmann celebrates after scoring just before half-time.

Teichmann sees the ball handled by Gillingham, André Joubert and Halstead before Justin Swart keeps up his impressive scoring record by going over, despite being on his knees, in the corner.
In complete control the Sharks start to play some expansive rugby but to their credit the Cheetahs are still very physical and putting in some big tackles as they attempt to stem the flow of constant Shark attacks.
Craig Davidson comes on to replace Hentie Martens and within minutes dives through the middle of a ruck to score after a big driving run from John Smit. The exuberant Davidson try celebration has already become something of a trademark.
Five minutes later the Sharks follow up with probably the best try of the game. On defence in their own 22 Halstead rips the ball from an attacker before accelerating through three tackles to launch a counter-attack. He makes it to the Cheetahs 22 before being run down. He off-loads to Clinton van Rensburg who in turn finds André Joubert who has a clear run in.
There is still enough time left for replacement flank Warren Britz to go over from a couple of yards before the Cheetahs finally get a try in the final minute of the game.
The mood afterwards is one of quiet satisfaction and restrained celebration. They have already started mentally preparing for next weeks final against the Golden Lions.]

Top Right: *Fly-half Clinton van Rensburg makes a break.*
Right:
The midfield defence was solid all night. Joe Gillingham puts in another big hit;
The back-line in perfect defensive alignment get ready to defend from a Cheetahs scrum;
The players walk back after their fourth try of the evening.

BISON
Canon

APPLETON
4
TEICHMANN
8
PAYNE
14

Left, from top:

The Sharks Springboks came back from the national camp to watch the game. Adrian Garvey (left) is captivated by the action on the field, while Mark Andrews, as usual, has some advice to give;

Loud and jovial before the game this group of Cheetahs supporters had already lapsed into sullen silence by half-time;

John 'Slugger' Slade, cheered on by Adrian Garvey and Etienne Fynn has a drink to celebrate his 100th Sharks cap after the game.

Right: *Hentie Martens and Justin Swart celebrate reaching the Currie Cup final while Steve Atherton watches the action in a pensive mood.*

Final

vs Lions

***The Sharks 9 vs Golden Lions 32**, The Stadium Kings Park, Durban, 11 September*
***Natal Sharks:** Joubert, Payne, Halstead, Gillingham, Swart, van Rensburg CI, Martens, Teichmann, Fyvie, Slade, Atherton, van Rensburg, Moyle, Visser, Smit*
***Golden Lions:** Englebrecht, Williams, vd Walt, Venter, Delport, Le Roux, Johnstone, Venter AJ, Minnaar, Strydom, Thorne, Labuschagne, Meyer, Boshoff, Mostert*

There is nothing like Cup Final day, whatever the sport. There has been an air of excitement around Durban all week. The match is sold out within hours of tickets going on sale. The match will be the last appearance in Sharks colours for Gary Teichmann and André Joubert, and will be Mac's last game too. Many are starting to believe that somehow victory has been pre-ordained.

Both have undoubtedly been the form sides of the competition so it is fitting they should meet in their fourth final of the decade. The Sharks lead 2-1 but both victories were at Ellis Park.

Both Mac and Lions coach Laurie Mains are highly respected and are used to success. In the run-up to Saturday they have nothing but good things to say about each other, their wariness and self-deprecation convincing but still unable to douse the competitive glint in their eyes.

Like the Sharks the Lions have been in irresistible form over the past couple of weeks. In their semi-final they scored over 80 points against the SWD Eagles, a side that beat the Sharks. Unlike their earlier visit to Durban their midfield maestro, Hennie Le Roux, is back at fly-half. Le Roux has been in outstanding form and is another player marginalised by Springbok management. He has sparked the Lions back-line into furious action with Bok discards Chester Williams and Thinus Delport in lethal form. At the heart of it all for the Lions is no 8 AJ Venter who has been inspirational all season.

> *"he's a legend"*
> *Lions coach Laurie Mains on Mac as the psychological warfare hots up before the final*

The Sharks have kept their routine the same and are thankful that there are no injury worries after the bruising semi-final. Another performance milestone will be reached by lock Steve Atherton as he joins assistant-coach Hugh Reece-Edwards as the most capped Natal Sharks player on 165 appearances.

The Sharks U19 and U21 teams are in the final of their respective competitions which act as curtain-raisers to the main game but both, somewhat ominously, lose.

In near perfect conditions the teams take the field. There is an excited over-wrought atmosphere and that is just in the press-box.

AJ Venter sets the tone with a huge hit on Halstead. The Sharks settle down quickly and pin the Lions back in their own half. André Joubert looks in the mood in his final game. His positioning is perfect and keeps the Sharks on the attack with probing kicks.

After five minutes Clinton van Rensburg kicks his first penalty, he bounces it in off the post the same as last week. A couple of minutes later he gets a second as the Sharks keep a grip on the game.

Despite dominating possession the Sharks aren't making it pay. Final passes go astray and there is a sudden rash of handling errors. The Lions put in some desperate defence and after 30 minutes there is a sense that the tide is turning.

On their first real attack the Lions set up good second-phase ball and move it quickly down the line. Crucially AJ Venter pops up in the centre and makes an overlap possible. His long pass finds Thinus Delport who brushes off a Joubert tackle to score in the corner.

The Lions come out after half-time playing inspired rugby. They thud into tackles and seem to have gained an extra yard of pace. Wickus Venter stays on his feet despite having three men holding into him before handing to Delport who scores in the corner again.

Five minutes later the Sharks try to get themselves back in the game with a degree of desperation. Martens' attempts to go blind but his pass is dropped and Chester Williams is on hand to kick through. He goes over virtually untouched and the game is over as a contest as the Lions take a 20-6 lead.

Gary Teichmann goes off with blood streaming from his head and Britz is on. The Sharks keep try-

Right: *André Joubert clears under pressure from Lions wing Thinus Delport.*

Below; from left:

Warming up underneath the main grandstand;
The keenly contested finals of the Visa mini-rugby tournament;
The bagpipes and a woman on a horse entertain the crowd before the main game;
Super-efficient Sharks PRO and top dancer Kim Davidson before the game, the woman's got balls;
The disappointed Sharks U21 side after losing their final.

Canon

Canon
GILBERT

THE STADIUM KINGS PARK

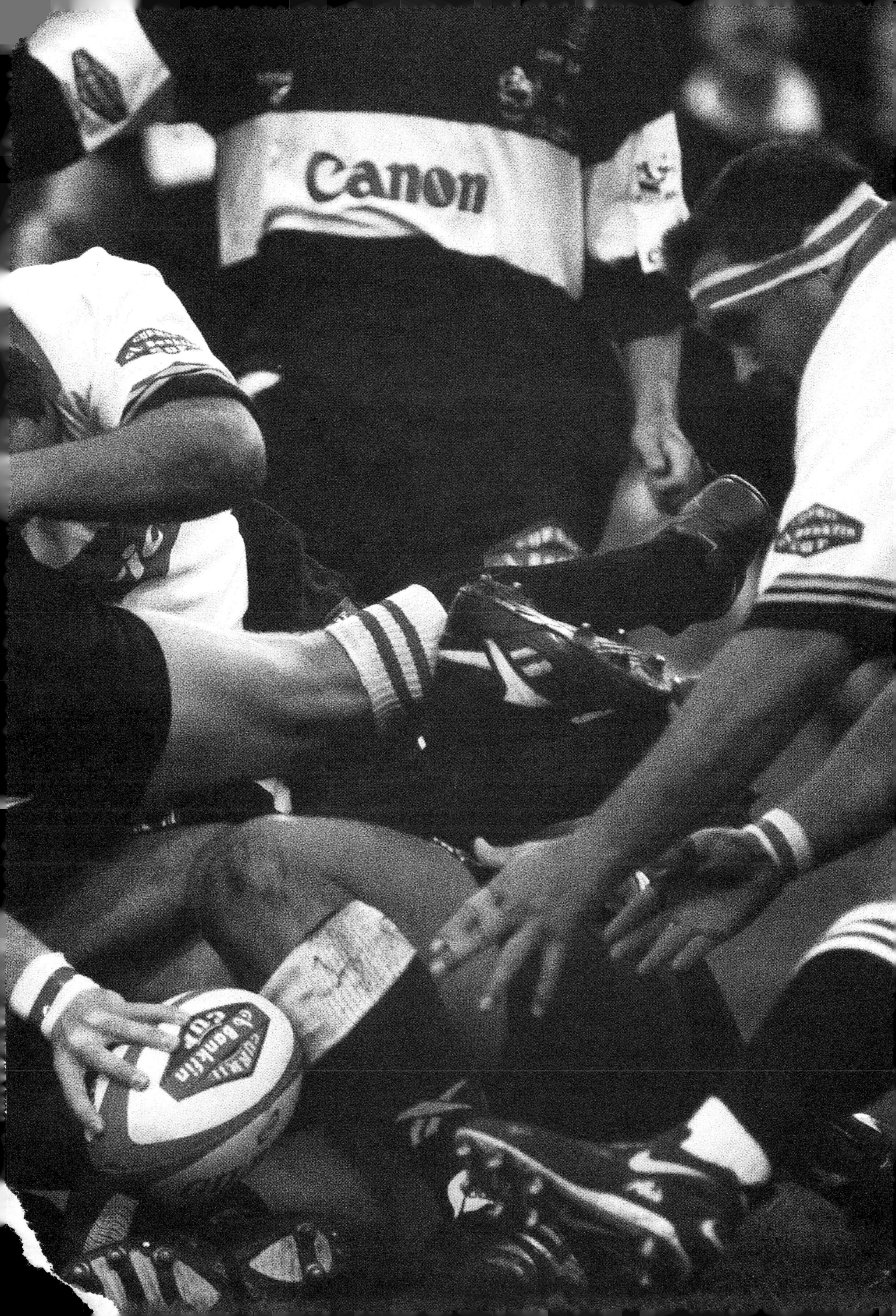
Canon

ing but there is a feeling of tired desperation about their play. The Lions give away a lot of penalties but the Sharks can't capitalise on the possession.

With two minutes remaining Lions prop Mostert scores before AJ Venter crowns his man-of-the-match performance with a final try. 32-9 is the Sharks worst defeat of the season but the Lions were clearly dominant and certainly deserved their victory.

The mood in the change room is muted but not despairing. The team desperately wanted to win for Mac but it wasn't to be. Mac as ever makes no excuses, though there is the feeling that perhaps bodies hadn't recovered sufficiently after the semi-final. "I just kept waiting for it to click, but it didn't,' says Trevor Halstead with a shrug.

André Joubert says farewell in the team huddle with a tear in his eye while young fly-half Clinton van Rensburg is inconsolable. Gary also gives a final pep talk: "Hold your heads high. You young guys have got a lot of talent and you will be back, this won't be your only final. I'll be watching you."

At the after-match function the great and the good of South African rugby gather for a quiet drink. The speeches from the captains are a highlight. The Lions' Hannes Strydom gives an eloquent heart-felt speech paying tribute to his own team but especially the departing Sharks trio.

Gary stands up for the last time as Sharks captain: "Unlike Hannes I haven't got anything prepared, I thought we were going to win."]

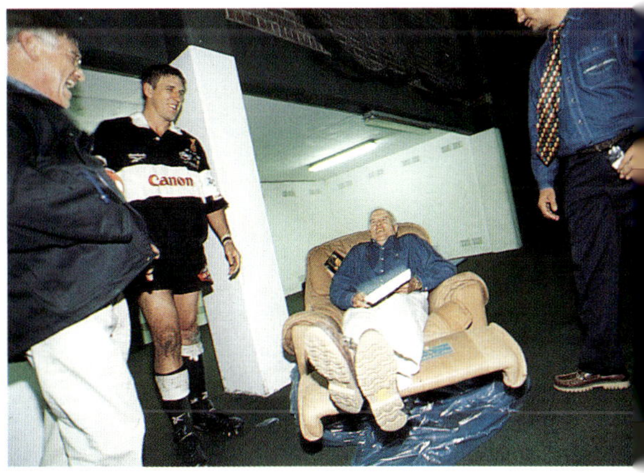

Left: *Moyle, Visser and Smit get ready to pack down.*

Right, from top:

Two great players meet for the last time. Gary Teichmann and Hennie Le Roux after the game;

As ever Joe Gillingham manages a smile as he signs autographs for the mascots in the change room;

The team gave Mac an easy chair as a retirement present, "Sit in it, watch television and don't even think about coming back," said Gary Teichmann.

Overleaf: *The last goodbye from Gary, Mac and André.*

MAC,
Reebok
Canon

TES
& ANDRÉ
Canon
RKS

Reebok

Many thanks to Ronald Coppin for getting the ball rolling.

To the players, Mac, Reece, Mike and the staff at the NRU, in particular Brian van Zyl, Peter Smith, Kim Davidson, Meryl Cleal, Terri Curtis, and Catherine and Caren on the front desk.

To Claire Clark, André du Plessis and Craig Irvine for their expertise and, more importantly, their support and belief.

To Mark Lanning for the occasional piece of valid advice and the image accompanying the introduction.

To Howard Cleland for kindly letting us use the image on page 24 , and his eccentric company on the touchline at many of the games.

To Karen and Mike Jander for their hospitality in Brisbane.

Sean Laurénz

Special thanks to my mother, Roselyn, Christopher and Liesl for their support and encouragement.

Paul Mitchell

To my girls, Wendy, Roma and Isabella. The weekends belong to you again.

Thanks to the Borthwicks of South Africa and Australia, the Melloys, Shirley and Kevin. Lastly, thank you John and Hazel for all your support and encouragement.

Sean Laurénz, is a freelance photojournalist whose editorial work appears in a variety of local and international publications.

Paul Mitchell is a full-time publisher, and an occasional freelance journalist.

For further information on Massive Publishing contact us at:
Box 37503, Overport, 4067, Durban,
South Africa.
Telephone: +27 31 207 8413
E-mail: massive@iafrica.com